Witchcraft
in America

Witchcraft
in America

Peggy Saari

Elizabeth Shaw, Editor

U·X·L®

AN IMPRINT OF THE GALE GROUP

DETROIT · SAN FRANCISCO · LONDON
BOSTON · WOODBRIDGE, CT

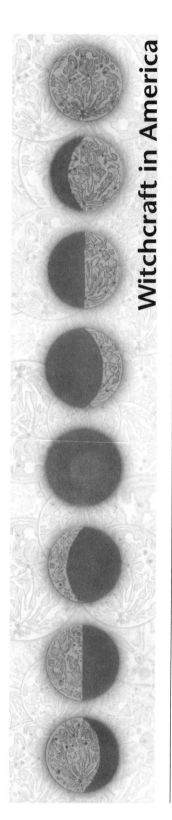

Witchcraft in America

Peggy Saari

Staff

Elizabeth M. Shaw, *U•X•L Associate Editor*
Allison McNeill, Bernard Grunow, *Contributing Editors*
Carol DeKane Nagel, *U•X•L Managing Editor*
Thomas L. Romig, *U•X•L Publisher*

Erin Bealmear, *Permissions Associate (Pictures)*
Maria Franklin, *Permissions Manager*
Kelly A. Quin, *Imaging and Multimedia Content Editor*

Rita Wimberley, *Senior Buyer*
Evi Seoud, *Assistant Manager, Composition Purchasing and Electronic Prepress*
Dorothy Maki, *Manufacturing Manager*
Mary Beth Trimper, *Production Director*

Michelle DiMercurio, *Senior Art Director*

Pamela A. Reed, *Imaging Coordinator*
Randy Basset, *Image Database Supervisor*
Barbara Yarrow, *Imaging and Multimedia Content Manager*

Linda Mahoney, LM Design, *Typesetting*

Cover photograph: Reproduced by permission of Mary Evans Picture Library.

Library of Congress Cataloging-in-Publication Data

Saari, Peggy.
 Witchcraft in America / Peggy Saari ; Elizabeth Shaw, editor.
  p. cm.
 Includes bibliographical references and index.
 ISBN 0-7876-4835-3 (hardcover)
 1. Witchcraft-United States- History- Juvenile literature. [1. Witchcraft-History.] I.
 Shaw, Elizabeth, 1973- II. Title.

 BF1573 .S23 2000
 133.4'3'0973-dc21   00-030264

Printed in the United States of America

10 9 8 7 6 5 4 3 2

Contents

Primary Sources

Biographies

Reader's Guide

Witchcraft in America is not a history of the practice of witchcraft. In fact, scholars have found no documented evidence of magic being performed by witches in America. Rather, this is a story about fear. European settlers who immigrated to the colonies in the early seventeenth century brought with them superstitions and beliefs, including the irrational fear of witches, that had accumulated over the course of many centuries in their home countries. As they set out across the Atlantic Ocean, witch-hunt hysteria was raging in Europe. After the colonists reached the shores of North America, they encountered an untamed wilderness where they struggled daily to survive the hardships of clearing the land and building communities. At this time science was a new and emerging field, and even well-educated people did not understand their world. Relying solely upon religion to show them the way in life, they were deeply afraid of forces that could not be explained as the will of God.

This was especially true of the Puritans, who had arrived in New England with a special mission to establish a perfect society. They believed that any adversity—epidemics, drought, crop failures, social unrest, political turmoil—was God's way of punishing them for their sins. Thus they feared God, and they came to fear one another, as existence in the New World became increasingly more difficult. Soon they were convinced that their problems would be solved if they rid themselves of witches, who were working in league with the devil to prevent the fulfillment of a harmonious community. Puritan officials in Salem, Massachusetts, held formal trials and executed nineteen innocent people for practicing witchcraft. The Salem trials left such an indelible mark on history that the term "witch-hunt" has entered the American vocabulary to describe the seeking out and hounding of people with unpopular or unconventional beliefs. Yet executions of suspected witches, all of them innocent, had taken place in New England before the Salem trials, and witchcraft superstitions lingered into the nineteenth century long after the executions had ended. Many of these same superstitions were revived, though in a different form, with the rise of Neo-Paganism in the 1970s. *Witchcraft in America* traces this story, from Europe in ancient times to modern America near the turn of the twenty-first century.

Features

Witchcraft in America offers a complete view of witchcraft using three separate formats-overview essays, primary source documents, and biographies. The six overview essays focus on such topics as witch-hunts in Puritan New England and the rebirth of Neo-Paganism in the twentieth century. The primary source section includes thirteen excerpts from documents such as *Malleus Maleficarum,* the book that started the European witch hunts; and "The Apology of Samuel Sewall," the public apology by a judge for his role in the Salem witch trials. Ten biographical essays highlight prominent figures related to the Salem witch trials, including Bridget Bishop, the first person hanged as a result of the Salem witch trials, and the woman believed to have planted the seed of hysteria in the Salem community, Carib slave Tituba. The book also has a timeline of events, a page of sources for further reading and research, and a section of research and activity ideas. There are more than 50 black-and-white photographs to enhance the text. Entries contain sidebars of information that further highlight the subject matter, and help define the context for some

of the events and people discussed, as well as definitions for
hard to understand words. The volume concludes with a subject index, so students can easily find the people, places, and
events discussed throughout *Witchcraft in America*.

Comments and Suggestions

We welcome your comments on *Witchcraft in America*. Please
write, Editors, *Witchcraft in America*, U•X•L, 27500 Drake
Road, Farmington Hills, MI 48331-3535; call toll-free: 1-800-
877-4253; fax to 248-414-5043; or send e-mail via
http://www.galegroup.com.

Research and Activity Ideas

Activity 1: Living history—witch hysteria in colonial America

    Assignment: Your social studies class has been selected to create a "living history" presentation on witch hysteria in colonial America. Your presentation will be featured in a school program, that will be attended by fellow students, parents, and members of the community. You have been asked specifically not to re-enact the Salem witch trials because most people know about these events. Instead, your project is to depict life in colonial America prior to the witch-hunts, focusing on factors that contributed to an environment of fear and suspicion. You will determine the format of your presentation, but you are expected to make it informative, involve all members of the class, and engage the imagination of the audience.

    Preparation: The first task is to hold a class discussion and choose the topics you will cover in your presentation. Possibilities include customs, superstitions, and social circumstances that contributed to witch hysteria in seventeenth-century colonial America. Another important factor would be the witch-hunts in Europe, which influenced settlers who moved to the American colonies. Once you have decided on the topics, you need to gather information. A convenient method is to select teams of four or five students who will do research on one particular topic. Using *Witchcraft in America* as a starting point, the teams must find information at the library and on Internet Web sites. Search for sources such as historians' accounts and documents from the period. Focus on little-known or especially interesting facts.

Presentation: After the teams have completed their research, the next step is to decide how to present the information. Decisions can be made either by the teams or by the class as a whole. Possible forms of presentation could be readings of excerpts from documents such as the *Malleus Malificarum,* the book that ignited the witch-hunts in Europe. Other possibilities include dramatizations of witch-hunts, audio-visual displays of illustrations from books, and demonstrations of witches' healing potions. To enhance the "living history" aspect of the presentation, team members can wear colonial-period clothing and adopt such roles as officials in charge of witch-hunts, accused witches, and townspeople. The final step is to prepare a fifty-minute presentation that will take your audience back to the time before the Salem witch trials and help them understand why the witch-hunts took place.

Activity 2: A teenager's view of the Salem witchcraft trials
Assignment: Imagine that you are a teenager who has been keeping a diary about life in Salem, Massachusetts, at the time of the witchcraft trials. You have a particular interest in the trials because you are a close friend of some of the girls who have accused local residents of being witches. The girls often told you about their involvement in the events that led to their accusations, and you recorded these details in your diary. You have also been attending the trials and keeping a record of their testimony. When the trials are over, you decide to write a final entry in which you give your views about why the witch-hunts took place, whether your friends told the truth, and whether justice was served. You plan to keep the diary and share it someday with your children.

Preparation: Your assignment is to compile several diary entries in which you describe: (1) what your friends told you, (2) what they said in court, and (3) your opinion of the trials. To complete these tasks, you must first select at least two friends who will be the focus of the diary entries. For instance, you might choose Ann Putnam, Jr., and Mary Warren, both of whom played a significant role in the trials. Next, using *Witchcraft in America* as a starting point, find additional information about the trials, focusing especially on your friends' involvement. After you have completed your research, write the entries specified above. You can expect your diary to be about three to five typewritten pages in length.

Presentation: Now, switch roles. Imagine that you have found the diary in a trunk in your grandmother's attic, and then discover that it was written by one of your ancestors. Take the diary to school and read it to your social studies class, which has just completed a unit on witchcraft in America.

Activity 3: Modern-day witch-hunts

Assignment: Your history class is completing a unit on social issues in twentieth-century America. The teacher has distributed a list of topics for independent projects that will enable you to learn more about one of those issues. You have chosen the topic of modern-day "witch-hunts," specifically a comparison of the Salem witch trials with the McCarthy hearings of the 1950s. The teacher has encouraged you to find additional examples of modern-day witch-hunts. The project will involve conducting research, writing a paper, and presenting an oral report to the class.

Preparation: The first step is to gather information about the Salem witch trials that you will use as a basis for your comparative analysis. It is essential at this stage to define the term "witch-hunt" that you will apply to modern-day events. Using *Witchcraft in America* as a starting point, find material in the library and on Internet Web sites that will help you state a definition and provide a frame of reference. Next, searching further in the library and on the Internet, gather information about the McCarthy hearings. At this point you may want to expand the scope of your topic by adding a more recent example of a modern-day witch-hunt. For instance, you might examine newspaper stories about Neo-Pagans and Wiccans to see if these groups can be considered victims of a witch-hunt. Once you have completed your research, write a paper at least five pages in length.

Presentation: Your teacher has requested that, after you have completed your paper, you make a photocopy for each person in the class. Then you are to present a five- or ten-minute oral report to the class, summarizing the results of your research. At the end of the report you will lead a brief discussion of the modern-day witch-hunts you have described in your paper and report.

Words to Know

A

Acute: severe.

Amnesty: pardon.

Anthropology: study of people and societies.

Apparition: ghostly figure.

B

Bigot: an extremely prejudiced person.

C

Calamity: disaster.

Charm: words, actions, or objects that are supposed to have magical powers.

Christianity: religion based on the teachings of Jesus Christ.

Compensation: payment.

Coven: a group of witches.

Culprit: person or thing responsible for something, usually bad.

D

Deity: a god or goddess.

Devastation: being physically or mentally destroyed.

Diameter: the measurement around a circle.

Disciple: follower.

Discontent: unhappiness.

Disobedient: not obeying the rules.

Druid: a group of pagan priests originating in ancient Britain.

E

Eccentric: odd or unique way of acting.

Elicit: to draw out.

Embellish: add to in an exaggerated way.

Epidemic: severe outbreak, usually of disease.

Eradication: destruction.

F

Famine: when there is not enough for everyone to eat.

Fertility: ability to have children.

Frail: fragile.

G

Gallows: a raised stand where hangings occurred.

Gruesome: disgusting.

H

Hallmark: a distinguishing characteristic.

Hamlet: small village.

Heathen: non-Christians.

Heresy: a belief that strays from the common beliefs of a religion.

Hysteria: panic often brought on by fear.

I

Indentured servant: one who signs a contract to work for an employer for a specified length of time.

Islam: a religion that believes in one God, and believes that the last prophet of that God was Muhammad.

J

Jeer: making fun of.

Judaism: a religion whose followers believe in one God and who follow the teachings of the Old Testament of the Bible and the Talmud, not the teachings of Jesus Christ.

Jurisdiction: area of judicial coverage.

L

Landmark: a landmark court decision is a decision that changes the way things are done, or changes the way a law is written.

M

Magic: the use of means believed to have supernatural power over natural forces.

Magistrate: an official of the courts; a judge.

Malevolent: evil.

Midwife: a woman trained to help a woman during childbirth.

Misogyny: an unfounded fear or hate of women.

Monotheism: the belief in one god.

Motive: reason.

Mythology: folklore.

N

Neo-Pagan: a person interested in reviving paganism.

Notorious: well-known for something bad.

O

Offspring: children.

Optimism: belief that the future holds good things.

Outwit: outsmart.

P

Pact: a verbal or written agreement.

Pagan: a person without religion.

Pardon: excuse.

Phenomenon: unusual event, thing or person.

Polytheism: the belief in many gods.

Potion: a mixture of liquid ingredients that is believed to have medicinal or magical powers.

Priest or **priestess:** spiritual leader.

Psychoanalyst: person who studies human minds.

R

Rationalism: beliefs based on facts, reason, and logic.

Rebuked: strongly criticized.

Reclusive: preferring to be alone.

Reign: rule.

Reinterpretation: another way of seeing or examining something.

Relic: an object with religious or historical significance.

Reprieve: pardon.

Resurgence: to become popular again.

Rivalry: competition.

S

Scapegoat: someone or something that is blamed for everything rather than the person or thing that is really at fault.

Scrutiny: careful inspection.

Shaman: a member of an organized society who acts as a spiritual leader or link between the physical world and the spiritual world..

Sorcerer: a wizard.

Specter: ghostly figure.

Spell: word or phrase that is believed to have magical powers.

Spiteful: being mean simply for the sake of being mean.

Sterility: inability to have children.

Stigma: a mental feeling of shame.

Strife: suffering.

Supernatural: otherworldly.

Superstition: belief in something with no factual basis.

T

Testimonial: sworn statement.

Totem: an object, usually an animal or plant, that serves as the symbol of a certain family or clan.

W

Wicca: witch.

Witch: a woman who is believed to be able to perform magic.

Timeline of Events in Witchcraft in America

15,000 B.C. Ancient peoples revere healers, known as witches, who practice magic.

600 A.D. Christian pope Gregory the Great proclaims "all the gods of the heathens are demons."

1200s Christianity has replaced traditional religions, which Christians call paganism.

1300s Women are singled out as witches in Europe.

1484 Pope Innocent VIII issues an edict that calls for the eradication of witches and other heathens.

1216
The Dominicans, the Order of Preachers, is founded.

1453
Gutenberg prints the first Bible. It is only 42 lines long.

1536
William Tyndale is strangled and burned at the stake. He was the first to translate the Bible into English.

1200	1400	1600

1486 *Malleus Maleficarum* (*Hammer of Witches*) triggers witch-hunts in Europe.

1580–1660 The war against witches reaches a peak in Europe.

1639 The Putnams start a land feud with the Townes near Topsfield, Massachusetts.

1647 Alse Young is executed as a witch in Wethersfield, Connecticut.

mid 1600s Ninety-three people are accused of witchcraft—fifty in Massachusetts and forty-three in Connecticut. Sixteen are put to death.

1684 The English government revokes the Massachusetts colonial charter.

Massachusetts minister Increase Mather publishes *Remarkable Providences,* a handbook for identifying witches.

1687 Rebecca Clinton is convicted of being a witch in Ipswich, Massachusetts.

1689 Samuel Parris is ordained as minister of the Salem village congregation.

1692 Witchcraft accusations begin at the Parris household.

January Betty Parris and Abigail Williams try a voodoo fortune-telling experiment. They begin having fits.

February Ann Putnam, Jr., Elizabeth Hubbard, and other Salem village girls join Betty Parris and Abigail Williams in having fits. They accuse Parris household slave Tituba, Sarah Good, and Sarah Osborne of casting spells on them.

March 1– 5 Tituba, Sarah Good, and Sarah Osborne are brought before judges.

1638
Anne Hutchinson is forced to leave the Massachusetts Bay Colony because of her outspoken nature and religious beliefs.

1647
George Fox founded the Religious Society of Friends (Quakers).

1661
John Eliot published the Bible in Algonkian, a Native American language.

1675
The Edict of Nantes is revoked, making Protestantism illegal again in France.

| 1630 | 1650 | 1670 |

March 6–19 The girls accuse Martha Corey of bewitching them. Betty Parris is sent to live in the home of Stephen Sewall.

March 21 Martha Corey is questioned and sent to jail.

March 21–23 Ann Putnam, Sr. begins having fits. She and the girls accuse Rebecca Towne Nurse of putting a spell on them.

March 24 Rebecca Nurse is questioned and sent to jail.

April 30 Thomas Putnam has joined in the accusations. Twenty-three accused witches have been jailed.

May 14 Puritan minister Increase Mather and the new Massachusetts governor, William Phips, arrive in the colony with a new charter from England.

May 31 Thirty-nine other people have been jailed as suspected witches.

June 2 Governor Phipps appoints the Court of Oyer and Terminer to try accused witches. Deputy governor William Stoughton is the chief judge. Bridget Bishop is convicted of witchcraft and sentenced to death.

June 10 Bridget Bishop is hanged. Nathaniel Saltonstall resigns from the panel of judges.

June 29 Sarah Good, Rebecca Nurse, Susannah Martin, Elizabeth Howe, and Sarah Wildes are put on trial. Although Nurse is acquitted, the judges ask the jury to review their decision; return a guilty verdict. Governor Phipps gives Nurse a reprieve, but later withdraws it. All the women are sentenced to death.

July 19 Sarah Good, Rebecca Nurse, Susannah Martin, Elizabeth Howe, and Sarah Wildes are hanged.

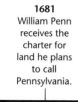

1681
William Penn receives the charter for land he plans to call Pennsylvania.

1688
William and Mary take the throne in England. Puritans are free to establish their own churches.

1693
Increase Mather writes *Cases of Conscience Concerning Evil Spirits*, about how wrong it was to accept spectral evidence in witchcraft trials.

1698
The first public library opens in Charleston, South Carolina.

1680   1690   1700

August 19 George Burroughs, John Procter, John Willard, George Jacobs, and Martha Carrier are hanged. Elizabeth Procter receives a reprieve because she is pregnant.

September 19 Giles Corey is pressed to death.

September 22 Martha Corey, Mary Easty, Alice Parker, Mary Parker, Ann Pudeator, Margaret Scott, Wilmot Redd, and Samuel Wardell are hanged.

October 3 Increase Mather gives a sermon in which he questions the validity of spectral evidence. The sermon is later published as *Cases of Conscience concerning Evil Spirits Personating Men.*

October 12 Governor Phipps forbids the jailing of more suspected witches.

October 29 Governor Phipps dissolves the Court of Oyer and Terminer.

November The "bewitched" Salem girls are called to Gloucester to identify witches, but they are ignored when they have fits.

1693 Cotton Mather publishes *Wonders of the Invisible World* in defense of the witch trials.

January 3 A Superior Court, headed by William Stoughton, is formed to try accused witches. After three are found guilty, Phipps gives them a reprieve; he also gives reprieves to five others sentenced previously.

January 31 Stoughton resigns from the court in protest against the reprieves.

May Governor Phipps orders all remaining accused witches released from jail after payment of their fees.

1706
Francis Makemie
founds the first
Presbytery in America
in Philadelphia

1731
Benjamin Franklin starts the
first circulating library in
Philadelphia.

1741
New England theologian
Jonathan Edwards delivered
the famous sermon "Sinners in
the Hands of an Angry God."

| 1710 | 1735 | 1760 |

1697

January 14 The Massachusetts General Assembly declares a Day of Fasting to commemorate the victims of the trials. Twelve trial jurors sign a statement admitting they convicted and condemned people to death on the basis of insufficient evidence. Salem trial judge Samuel Sewall makes a public apology for his role in the executions.

Robert Calef writes *More Wonders of the Invisible World,* in which he attacks accusers and judges in the Salem trials.

Samuel Parris is forced to resign as minister of the Salem village church.

1703 The Reverend Joseph Green formally reverses Martha Corey's excommunication from Salem village church.

1706 Ann Putnam, Jr. makes an apology for her role in sending innocent people to their deaths.

1710 The Massachusetts General Court grants the sum of 578 pounds as compensation to the families of Salem trial victims.

early 1700s The Enlightenment begins to displace Puritanism and traditional superstitions.

1782 The last European witchcraft execution takes place in Switzerland.

1800 Belief in witchcraft lingers in New England.

1846 American writer Nathaniel Hawthorne writes *Young Goodman Brown,* one of many stories and novels about Puritan bigotry and repression.

1773
The first black Baptist church is founded in America in Silver Bluff, South Carolina

1791
The First Amendment was drafted to protect the freedom of religious choice.

1820
Joseph Smith founds the Church of Jesus Christ of Latter-Day Saints.

1785   1810   1835

early 1900s The British Order of the Druids revives the practice of Wicca.

1921 British archaeologist Margaret Murray writes *The Witch-Cult in Europe,* sparking an interest in witch covens.

1951 Anti-witchcraft laws of 1735 are repealed by the British Parliament. English writer Gerald B. Gardner declares himself a witch.

1960s Neo–paganism spreads throughout North America and Europe.

1975 The Covenant of the Goddess is formed to incorporate hundreds of separate Wiccan covens. It is officially recognized as a church in the United States.

1985 The District Court of Virginia declares that Wicca is a legitimate religion protected by the First Amendment.

1999 A Wiccan vernal equinox celebration starts a controversy at Fort Hood, Texas.

1918
A deadly influenza epidemic grips world and an estimated 40 million people die.

1925
Scope's Monkey Trial brings national attention to Fundamentalism

1947
The House Committee on Un-American Activity starts what is later called a "witch-hunt," trying to uncover Communists in the United States.

1998
A series of children's books about a boy becoming a wizard takes the United States by storm.

1900   1950   2000

Almanac

Witchcraft in Europe

Long before religions based on a belief in one god, such as Judaism, Christianity, and Islam, became the dominant religions of the world, most cultures believed in more than one god, or were polytheistic. At the center of this ancient belief system was the idea that the world is controlled by powers that are both visible and invisible, and people relied on magic—the use of means believed to have supernatural power over natural forces—to understand and control their environment. Archaeologists, scientists who study the remains of ancient cultures, and scholars have discovered cave drawings dating back as far as 17,000 years that depict the practice of magic. In an ancient community one or two people possessed the wisdom and skill to work magic, which involved making potions and casting spells to bring about certain effects or events. They predicted the future, gave advice, and interpreted the will of unknown spiritual forces. They concocted herb remedies for pain and disease, assisted in the birthing of children, and were relied upon for success in hunting and growing crops.

People with these special skills, which were considered sacred, were granted a high moral and social status. Most were

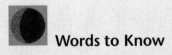

Words to Know

charm: words, action,s or objects that are supposed to have magical powers

Christianity: religion based on the teachings of Jesus Christ

deity: a god or goddess

druid: a group of pagan priests originally in ancient Britain

eradication: destruction

famine: state when there is not enough for everyone to eat

fertility: ability to have children

heathen: non-Christians

heresy: a belief that strays from the common teachings of a religion

hysteria: panic often brought on by fear

Islam: a religion that believes in one God, and believes that the last prophet of that God was Muhammad

Judaism: a religion whose followers believe in one God and do not follow the teachings of Jesus, but rather the Old Testament of the Bible and the Talmud

magic: the use of means believed to have supernatural power over natural forces

midwife: a woman trained to help a woman during childbirth

misogyny: an unfounded fear or hate of women

monotheism: the belief in one god

pagan: a person without religion

polytheism: the belief in many gods

potion: a mixture of liquid ingredients that has medicinal or magical powers

relic: an object with religious or historical significance

shaman: a member of an organized society who acts as a spiritual leader or link between the physical world and the spiritual world

sorcerer: a wizard

spell: a word or phrase that is believed to have magical powers

supernatural: other worldly

superstition: belief in something with no factual basis

totem: an object, usually an animal or plant, that serves as the symbol of a certain family or clan

witch: a woman who is believed to be able to perform magic

women, but many men also possessed the knowledge to alter events through supernatural and natural means. Nevertheless women were believed to have a direct connection with unseen forces through their ability to bear children and thus influence the continuity of life. Many modern historians consider this era to have been a life–affirming time in human history, when

Magic, Witchcraft, and Sorcery

Whether magic is used for productive or destructive purposes, it consists of four elements. The first is the use of symbolic gestures and ritualized behavior, which could involve dancing, singing, or any number of motions believed to bring about a desired outcome. Every culture on Earth contains some aspect of symbolic gestures or ritualized behavior performed either by an entire group or by a select few individuals. Another element is the use of particular objects and/or substances that produce magical effects. Among them are totems (emblems), powders, charms, and herbal mixtures. Contemporary scientists have actually conducted research with substances commonly used by ancient practitioners of magic. The scientists found that the substances could induce intense feelings of power and transformation. In one case, ingredients for a "flight potion" from the thirteenth century were mixed by two scientists who independently reported that they felt they had flown to the top of a high mountain and spoken with spirits. A third part of magic is a special utterance or series of words that are believed to carry significant power. The final element involves the qualities possessed by the performer of rituals. Each culture had its own definition of the person who was capable of performing magic, whether it be the shaman, village midwife, or council of druids. Only a select few were trusted—and even feared—for their ability to enter the unique mental and physical state necessary to perform magic.

During ancient times a distinction was made between sorcerers and witches. Both were considered to have the power to influence events through the use of magic, but sorcerers were feared more than witches. Acting in malevolent and spiteful ways, sorcerers performed what was called "black magic." On the other hand, witches used "white magic" for the benefit of their communities. They were regarded as valuable and necessary members of society up until the beginning of the Middle Ages. The distinction between sorcerers and witches was finally erased by the Christian movement, which equated any form of magical practice with Satanism and evil.

women held a special place in the community. Eventually people with magical skills came to be known as witches. The term "witch" has been traced to Old Teutonic (Germanic) words like *wik* (meaning to bend) or Old English words such as *wiccian* (to cast spells) and *witan* (wise person). The use of magic for beneficial purposes was even encouraged by the Old Testament (the first part of the Bible, the Christian holy book), which demanded the death penalty for practitioners of malevolent (evil) magic but acknowledged the positive virtues of "white" (beneficial and healing) magic.

Christianity slowly takes over

As Christianity (a religion founded by Jesus of Nazareth, also called the Christ) became the prevalent religion in Europe, ancient traditions were increasingly pushed toward the fringes of society. At the beginning of the transition period, however, there was minimal conflict between Christians and those who continued traditional practices. In fact, traditional practices were often combined with Christian rituals (religious ceremonies). The first converts to Christianity were people who belonged to the upper classes and the nobility. Thus being a Christian became a sign of high social and political status. Peasants and members of the lower class, known as "pagans" (from the ancient Latin word for peasant or country dweller), were generally left to practice their versions of the old religion as long as they posed no threat to the church and ruling class. Over time non–Christian beliefs came to be called "paganism" by the Christians. Although Christians built churches directly on top of significant pagan worship sites, in the early years they did not devote significant money or energy to converting inhabitants in rural regions. Often craftsmen hired to build the new churches were non–Christians who incorporated aspects of the old religion into the new. For instance, they left carvings of horned gods and fertility goddesses (pagan images of life–giving forces) inside these new monuments.

Paganism and Christianity were blended in other ways. Two altars (worship centers) were erected side by side in some Christian churches so that worshipers could make offerings to both Christ and various pagan gods simultaneously. As late as the thirteenth century many Christian priests continued leading their congregations in fertility dances (to influence success in conceiving children) and practicing magic in private. Early laws discouraged the practice of pagan religions throughout Europe. Yet these were relatively lenient attempts to gradually wean the people from their so–called superstitions rather than a calculated campaign to eliminate paganism. In A.D. 600 the Christian pope (the supreme head of the church),

Witches Apprehended, Examined and Executed, for notable villanies by them committed both by Land and Water.

With a strange and most true triall how to know whether a woman be a Witch or not.

Printed at London for *Edward Marchant*, and are to be sold at his shop ouer against the Crosse in Pauls Church-yard. 1 6 1 3.

Gregory the Great (540–604), proclaimed that "all the gods of the heathens are demons" and should be punished. That message did not take root until several hundred years later.

Setting the stage for "The Burning Times"

Between the twelfth and fifteenth centuries Christians came to see paganism as a major threat to the church.

By this time the positive and honorable aspects of the old religions had been redefined to appear both destructive and evil. Ironically, witches who were once instrumental in guaranteeing continued fertility, good health, and plentiful harvests were suddenly held responsible for sterility, disease, infant mortality, famine, and blight. One reason for this shift was that the monotheism (belief in one god) of Christianity was in direct opposition to the old notion of multiple gods and natural forces at work in a mysterious universe (polytheism). The nature–based pagan approach to life was displaced by rigid allegiance to the one all–knowing God and the one "true" religion, Christianity. Now the focus was on life after death—the Christian concept of heaven (paradise) and hell (eternal suffering)—rather than human existence on Earth. Church leaders declared that any form of worship or spiritual power other than Christianity was related to the devil. This narrow view allowed little room for pagan beliefs and the mysterious healing practices of witches. Since the church could not dismiss the fact that healers held some authentic power in pagan communities, Christian officials simply declared that witches were doing the devil's work. In other words, the Christians reasoned that if healers were not receiving their power from the church, they must be getting it from the devil, who used them to commit evil. This was also a time in history when people believed that humans were on Earth to suffer for God. Anyone who could relieve suffering was thought to be working against the will of God and collaborating with evil forces. Witches were thus anti–Christian and therefore needed to be destroyed.

New systems replace old ways

The witch craze was also fueled by serious social, economic, and political changes taking place across Europe. For instance, the bubonic plague, a widespread contagious disease that raged for about twenty years beginning in 1334, killed nearly three-fourths of the populations of Europe and Asia. In addition, a large percentage of men had died in wars, leaving more women than men in many European countries. There was also a high infant death rate. At the same time, women were increasingly being viewed with suspicion for their role in

The Pagan Horned God Becomes the Devil

One of the main deities (gods) found throughout the pre–Christian world was the horned god. Known as the god of hunting, fertility, luck, and winter time (when hunting was the primary means of survival), he was referred to by many names, such as Pan, Dionyssus, or Bachus, to name a few. Various cultures worshiped this god through ceremonies in which antlers or horns were worn by participants prior to major hunting expeditions. Relics from and drawings of the ceremonies have been found all over the world, with the common factor always being the existence of horns from the main herding animals of the region. Many historians and archaeologists believe that Christianity took the symbols of the old religion and altered their meaning forever by creating the image of the devil. The replica of the old horned god was given the added characteristic wings of the fallen angel, or the devil, and other elements relating to the Christian belief in heaven and hell. Christianity in essence stole the horned god, who had symbolized positive aspects of humanity's relationship with nature, and made it into the very representation of evil on Earth and the greatest enemy known to God. Contemporary words for the devil have no basis in Christianity itself. In the Old Testament, the Hebrew term *Ha–Satan* simply means "an enemy." The same is true in the New Testament, in which the Greek word *diabolos* also means "an adversary." Ironically, witches did not even believe in the devil but they became closely and fatally associated with it through their connection to the old religion.

childbearing and for the mysterious functions of their bodies. Many rural healers and witches were unmarried women or widows who did not seem to fit into society, and church leaders became suspicious of the power they wielded in their communities. Some historians believe that misogyny (hatred of women) quickly replaced the old pagan respect for female qualities, as Christians came to associate women's sexuality and freedom with the work of the devil.

Simultaneously, the rise of the field of medicine, with its treatment of illness and disease through scientific methods—and which was exclusively upper class, Christian, and male—edged out competition from village healers and other so-called "heathens" (non-Christians), such as Jews. For exam-

As a strange hatred for women replaced the old pagan respect, women were being viewed with suspicion for things as innocent as childbearing. *Reproduced by permission of Culver Pictures.*

ple, Jews, followers of Judaism (a religion whose followers believe in one God and do not follow the teachings of Jesus, but rather the Old Testament of the Bible and the Talmud) were the only surgeons in Europe prior to this new movement. Eventually the medical establishment declared that it was illegal to perform any healing arts without "formal certification," thereby reducing traditional surgeons and healers to the status of criminals. Even village midwives who assisted in the birthing of babies were discredited and placed under deep suspicion.

Another factor was the new judicial system that arose in the twelfth century and considerably weakened the power of individuals and small communities. Prior to that time, the traditional legal system (known as *lex talionis*) had stated that an accuser must prove his or her accusation to be true or suffer the punishment that the defendant would have received if he were proven guilty. In other words, a person could not simply make an accusation with impunity (freedom from being punished if he were lying) but had to provide serious and concrete proof of a crime. The goal of the old system was community harmony and justice, and it discouraged the abuse of law and the courts. In contrast, the new system (which would play a major role in the witch craze) was based on Roman law and encouraged the use of heavy penalties, fines, punishments, and even death for those accused of major crimes. The goal was to protect the power and unification of the state and church rather than the small community. Depending on the status of the accused, it was sufficient in many cases for someone to be arrested and brought to trial simply on the basis of unproven charges.

Church targets "enemies" for elimination

The increased centralization—and focusing of power—of church and state called for the elimination of all "enemies" of the church, not just pagans and healers. In the thirteenth century the Catholic Church embarked on a judicial (law-oriented) campaign known as the Inquisition, which used both government and church to wipe out or convert heretics (nonbelievers) in western Europe. Before the onset of the witch craze, Jews were especially vulnerable, as were Muslims (followers of Islam), homosexuals, and Gypsies (wandering people who originated in India). Members of these targeted groups were driven to resettle in eastern and southern Europe. Many of the same accusations that later fueled the hysteria against witches were initially aimed at these peoples. Charged with making pacts with the devil, eating children, and murdering Christians, they were often tortured to the point of confessing to crimes they did not commit. The word *synagogue* (a Jewish place of worship) was actually redefined to describe a time and place of devil worship. The word *Sabbath,* traditionally associated with the Jewish day of rest, came to symbolize large group meetings between witches and the devil. Even the stereotype of a witch was borrowed from the racist caricature (distorted representation of certain physical features) of Jews and Arabs as having extremely large, crooked noses. These were but a few ways in which differences were transformed into concrete fears.

Though Jews, Muslims, homosexuals, and Gypsies were not actually a political threat, they were used by church and government officials to stir up suspicion and violence during the

Inquisition. Thus Christian leaders gained supremacy through growing bigotry and intolerance toward "outsiders" or anyone else who might threaten the status quo (the existing state of affairs). This campaign caused great fear among the common people, preparing the way for the persecution of witches. Witchcraft had been added to the list of official punishable heresies (beliefs that go against the teachings of the church) in 1320, but witches did not become a primary target for more than a century.

Then in 1484 Pope Innocent VIII (1432–1492) issued a Papal Bull (an edict or proclamation) that called for the eradication of witches and other heathens. Although many such edicts had previously been issued, the Papal Bull of 1484 had the advantage of a recent invention, the printing press, which spread anti-witch hysteria like wildfire throughout Europe.

Malleus Maleficarum triggers horrors

As the result of mass production made possible by the printing press, the second-best-selling book in Europe for more than two centuries was the *Malleus Maleficarum* (*Hammer of Witches*; see primary sources entry). This three-part work was the official handbook for detecting, capturing, trying, and executing witches. It was written in 1486 by Austrian priest Heinrich Kramer (also spelled Kraemer; 1430–1505) and German priest Jakob Sprenger (c. 1436–1495) at the request of Pope Innocent VIII. An especially frightening impact of the *Malleus* was that it united the church and the state, making horrific torture perfectly legal as a means of obtaining "confessions" from accused witches.

One of the most common means of torture was the stretching rack, a device that would slowly tear a person limb from limb as he or she was repeatedly commanded to confess to specific crimes. A similar tool was the strapado, which involved attaching weights to a victim's legs, then slowly lifting the person off the ground so that the legs would begin to tear out. Another method involved the victim being stripped naked and slowly cut in half by being dragged along a very tight rope. Some people were tied to stakes and placed near a fire that would very slowly "cook" them. Many others had their eyes gouged out or were beaten, raped, disemboweled (having ones internal organs cut out), dropped from high above the ground, or subjected to numerous devices created specially for the task. Also popular were "Spanish Boots," which were put on a victim's legs and could work in either of two ways: one used internal vices that would slowly crush the victim's legs, while the other involved pouring boiling water or oil into the "boots."

These methods were extremely efficient. People were brought close to death and promised relief if they confessed to the charges against them. Thousands gave in, no matter how fabricated or ridiculous the charges might have seemed, to save themselves from further torture. In turn, the "confessions" fanned mass hysteria, "proving" that the initial suspicions had been correct and creating an enemy out of innocent people. Officials in some regions used "tests" that pointed to the guilt of an accused person in various inevitable ways. One that was extremely popular in England (where torture was considered a crime) was the water test. The results were supposed to determine whether a person was indeed a witch—yet nobody could actually "pass" the test. It involved tying the accused person's arms and legs together, then throwing him or her into a body of water. If the victim sank, he or she was not a witch and would be dealt with by God accordingly in heaven. Since multilayered clothing was worn at the time, people quite often ended up floating because their clothes created pockets of air that forced them to remain at the surface of the water. Many "witches" were declared guilty by this method, then publicly burned at a stake in the center of town. Burning was considered another test, as well as the most severe form of punishment: it was thought that witches could survive fire because of their association with the devil. The prevalence of the fire test led to this era being called "The Burning Times."

Malleus becomes basis for laws

Another cruel aspect of the witch-hunts was that relatives of the accused were charged money for all manner of details involved in the trial of their loved ones. Not only did they pay the salary of the judge/torturer, they also bore the cost of food and lodging for the accused in prison. In addition, relatives were charged for the wood and straw used for kindling the execution fire, and they were billed for the lavish banquets typically held for officials before mass executions. In the case of accused people who had no relatives in the region, personal property was confiscated to pay the bills. The result was that many people lost their land, money, and lives while a few witch-hunters and judges accumulated wealth with every successful trial.

According to the *Malleus*, "it has never yet been known that an innocent person has been punished on suspicion of

The Pope and the Authors

Historical records from the late 1400s help shed light on the characters responsible for the campaign against witches. Pope Innocent VIII, who issued the Papal Bull condemning witches in 1484, was known for his adamant position against all things relating to fertility and sexuality. For instance, he published edicts describing the few situations in which sexual activity could not be considered the work of the devil, thus setting unrealistic guidelines for the common people. Yet historians have learned that he had a long-term relationship with a woman who bore him two illegitimate children. It is also said that for several months he was kept alive on his deathbed by nursing from the breast of a grown woman, and he received blood transfusions that cost the lives of four young "donors."

Heinrich Kramer and Jakob Sprenger, authors of the anti-witch handbook *Malleus Maleficarum,* also left less than honorable records in the history books. One account says that Kramer once bribed an old woman to climb into a baker's oven and scream that the devil had put her there. She was then forced to accuse several people in the village of working for the devil, and they were all put to death. Kramer was notorious for relishing his power and authority over the lives of accused villagers. Sprenger is known to have forged an official letter of praise from the theological faculty (those teaching

Innocent VIII wanted greater control over the punishment of witches, so he had Heinrich Kramer and Jakob Sprenger write *Malleus Maleficarum.*
Reproduced by permission of Archive Photos, Inc.

religion) of the University of Cologne in support of the *Malleus Maleficarum.* This prestigious board was responsible for censoring and approving all publications throughout Europe, and the forged letter was included in every copy of the book except for editions sold in the city of Cologne itself. This fact remained hidden until 1898, when a German scholar uncovered evidence of Sprenger's trickery. Although it was not generally known at the time, Sprenger had such a poor reputation that his colleagues at the University of Cologne would not permit the traditional mass to be performed at his funeral.

witch-craft and there is no doubt that god would never permit such a thing to happen." The book became the guide for civil and church law for over two centuries, going through twenty-eight editions between 1486 and 1600. It was accepted by Catholics and Protestants alike as the authority on ridding Europe of satanism and witchcraft, which were now considered inseparable. The *Malleus* was both the catalyst and fuel for the intense panic and hatred that swept through Europe, resulting in what some have called genocide, the planned and systematic extermination of an entire group of people.

The extent of the witch craze

The war against witches reached its peak between 1580 and 1660, and officially ended on June 17, 1782, when the last execution took place in Switzerland. The hysteria raged mainly in France, Germany, and Switzerland, but also extended throughout western Europe, into pockets of northern and eastern Europe, and eventually to the American colonies in New England. Spain was one of the few countries not associated with the witch-hunts because Spanish officials did not believe in witchcraft as defined by the *Malleus*. In Spain "witches" were apparently dealt with by being locked up in convents. It is difficult to establish the number of people who were killed in the anti-witch campaign because many died in jails from torture and starvation and were not recorded in official execution counts. Estimates based on compilations of regional figures throughout Europe range anywhere from 100,000 to 9,000,000. The majority of those killed were not necessarily followers of the old religions but Christian men, women, and children who had been wrongfully accused. On average, 80 percent of the accused were women and 85 percent of those actually executed were women. Most men who were accused were either related to women who had been tried, or they had criminal records implicating them in other crimes against the church and state.

Records from specific regions help illuminate the full magnitude of these events. The most horrific and extreme measures were taken in Germany. At the start of the seventeenth century the ruling prince of western Germany established a huge team of prosecutors and torturers equipped with special buildings and devices made specifically for torture. In the city of Bamberg, for instance, officials burned nine hundred witches in the first half of the century alone. Three hundred of the victims were under the age of four. In the village of Langendorf all but two women were arrested as witches. Two other German villages were left with only one female inhabitant each. Records show that in nearby Alsace, a province in France, a total of five thousand people were burned during the witch-hunts.

England had its moments of severity as well, particularly after 1604, when King James I (1566–1625) passed a law that officially prohibited pacts with the devil. James stated publicly that out of every twenty-one witches, twenty were women, thus contributing to a focus on women as targets. In one case, after a particularly severe winter the Bishop of Treves executed the inhabitants of an entire village because he could not determine who was a witch. He decided to let God be the judge. Another Englishman named Matthew Hopkins made a fortune hunting down witches because he got paid for each conviction, not just for the number of accused. He was renowned for his intense torture sessions (before torture was outlawed in the country) and was single-handedly responsible for over 230 "convictions."

Although there were some vocal opponents of the witch craze throughout Europe, very few survived their own outspokenness. Most were considered guilty by association and were virtually powerless against the enormity of the campaign. By the end of the seventeenth century, however, two factors brought the persecutions to a halt. First, officials were running out of victims: so many people had been killed that entire regional populations had been altered. The high number of executions began raising concerns about the need to slow down. In response to the atrocities in Bamberg and other areas of Germany, Ferdinand II (1578–1637), the Holy Roman Emperor, issued a decree to stop the killings. Other officials slowed down the mechanisms of the campaign as they began to realize it was no longer necessary: in a sense, the war had been won and it was not particularly profitable to carry on the hunt. Another factor that helped grind the machine to a halt was a new European ideology (system of beliefs about the individual's place in society) that envisioned a more rational and ordered universe. This shift in thinking eventually led to the era called the Enlightenment that began in the eighteenth century. By then past history was dismissed as having been the result of irrational, ancient superstitions. People moved forward into a new age, choosing not to look back.

For Further Study

Barstow, Anne Llewellyn. *Witchcraze: A New History of teh European Witch Hunts*. San Francisco, California: harper, 1999.

Stern, Wendy. *Witches: Opposing Viewpoints*. San Diego, California: Greenhaven Press, 1995.

Wizards and Witches. Brendan Lehan and others, editors. Alexandria, Virginia: Time-Life Books; School and library distribution by Silver Burdett, 1984.

Witch-Hunts in Puritan New England

2

The witch trials that took place in Salem, Massachusetts, in 1692 and 1693 are remembered today as a tragic chapter in American history. The trials are generally considered to be a unique and isolated flare-up of European superstitions that had been brought to America by a few settlers. Yet a closer look at this era reveals that, from the very beginning, fear of witchcraft was a basic part of New England society and served many complex functions. Although belief in witchcraft was prevalent throughout the American colonies, formal trials and executions occurred only in the Puritan communities of New England, the northeastern part of the present-day United States. The reason was that the Puritans had a unique sense of their mission in America. They were originally members of Protestant groups in England that opposed practices of the Church of England under King James I (1566–1625). (Protestants belong to a religious group that was formed in opposition to the Roman Catholic Church in the late 1500s. Although the Church of England is a Protestant denomination [sect], many aspects of the doctrines [laws and teachings] and worship services are based on Roman Catholicism.) The Puritans condemned the use of religious

Words to Know

eccentric: odd or unique way of acting

epidemic: severe outbreak, usually of disease

gallows: a raised stand where hangings occurred

magistrate: an official of the courts

malevolent: evil

notorious: well-known for something bad

pact: a verbal or written agreement

phenomenon: unusual event

psychoanalyst: person who studies human minds

spiteful: being mean simply for the sake of being mean

sterility: inability to have children

testimonial: sworn statement

icons (images such as pictures and statues), written prayers, instrumental music, and other elements in worship services. Thus they had a reputation as troublesome and overly pious (religiously devout) people.

The Puritans' protests angered James I and his successor Charles I (1600–1649), both of whom forced them to leave England. After living in other European countries such as the Netherlands (Holland), the Puritans began arriving in New England in 1620. At that time Puritans calling themselves the Pilgrims founded the Plymouth colony in Massachusetts with hopes of establishing their vision of God's Kingdom on Earth. Nine years later another group of Puritans was given a charter (government deed) for starting the nearby Massachusetts Bay Colony. All the Puritans had intense faith in themselves as God's "chosen people." They also brought European superstitions regarding witchcraft and the inferiority of women, which became crucial factors in the "witch" persecutions of the late seventeenth century.

The devil among them

Since the Puritans saw themselves as God's chosen people, they believed they had been sent to the New World (the European term for North and South America) to wage a battle against the agents of the devil (the Christian term for the source of all evil). Consequently, they considered Native Americans, European settlers of different faiths, and the unpredictable forces of nature to be forms of the devil himself—and therefore direct challenges to the will of God. As soldiers in the war between good and evil, the Puritans established a highly structured society with rigid laws and rules based on the Christian holy book, the Bible. They viewed any sinful act as trea-

son against the entire community and an invitation to the devil. To avoid transgression (an act in violation of a law), the church tightly controlled every aspect of daily life. They prohibited any activities that opened the doors to sin, such as games, dancing, frequent bathing, physical recreation, and social gatherings outside of church. Anyone who deviated from the rules immediately aroused suspicion. Puritans were also disturbed by any signs of difference, which they inter-

The Fate of the Daughters of Eve

Women led difficult lives through out the American colonies, but the status of women was particularly low in New England Puritan communities. Puritan ministers used the biblical tale of Adam and Eve, the first man and woman God created, to show that women had inherited Eve's original sin—she was tempted to eat the forbidden fruit of knowledge—and could not be trusted. Puritans thought that women were the source of all problems on Earth, and that only men were capable of solving these problems. Yet entrance into heaven was predetermined by God for only a select few men, who would find out they were chosen after they died. While they were on Earth, however, they called themselves the "elect," or the Saints. The elect were at the center of Puritan religious and social life, and they were the only people permitted to join the church, become freemen (citizens), or vote. This did not mean that women did not have to go to church. In fact, church attendance was mandatory for everyone, and skipping worship services was a punishable crime. Women were therefore silent observers, often listening to sermons on the most popular topic of the day: women's inferiority as the result of Eve's sin.

preted as the presence of evil in their midst. For instance, they thought crippled, aged, poor, eccentric, deformed, and sickly people were possibly the offspring of Satan.

Puritan laws gave women as little freedom and power as possible. For example, a widow who tried to keep her dead husband's estate rather than pass it on to her sons was in danger of losing everything in court. A woman adulteress could be put to death for her crime. Puritans believed that women could gain access to power only through communion with the devil. For this reason strong-willed, independent, and unmarried women were most frequently targeted as witches. Many women became suspects simply because they were not part of the mainstream community.

The devil's favorite challenge

New England ministers preached that the devil had singled out Puritans for special challenges because they were the most dedicated opponents of evil on Earth. Furthermore, they believed that witches were human manifestations (embodiments) of the devil, and that the devil's favorite way of testing Puritans was to place witches in the heart of their communities. **Cotton Mather** (see biography and primary sources entries), the prominent Massachusetts Bay minister, expressed the typical view in *Wonders of the Invisible World* (1693), his famous book on "proofs" of witchcraft: "If any are scandalized that New England, a place of as serious piety as any I can hear of under Heaven should be troubled so much with witches, I think 'tis no wonder: where will the Devil show the most malice but where he is hated, and hateth, most?" As life in the New World became increasingly difficult, the Puritans began blaming witches for all of their problems—economic hardship, epidemic illnesses, political conflict, and social unrest. Eventually they decided that eliminating witches was the only way to achieve victory over the devil. As John Putnam Demos notes in *Entertaining Satan,* a history of the witchcraft trials: "Witches could be blamed for a good deal of trouble and difficulty. In this respect the belief in witchcraft was very useful indeed. To discover an unseen hand at work in one_s life was to dispel mystery, to explain misfortune, and to excuse incompetence." During the second half of the seventeenth century charges of witchcraft became rampant in Puritan communities.

The first witch trials in the New World

Unity against adversity

Modern historians have noted a repeated pattern throughout New England in the early 1600s: community conflict or stress had a direct relationship to accusations of witchcraft. In the first half of the century, Puritans worked hard to establish settlements under extremely adverse conditions in the wilderness of New England. The challenges of daily existence forced them to cooperate with one another. Yet at the same time they were exposed to constant tension and fear, which caused them to lash out at their neighbors. Internal squabbling, particularly about matters of faith and worship, split many Puritans into ever smaller and more remote communities with their own concepts about carrying out the true mission of God. These small settlements were even more vulnerable to the untamed wilderness, so they were focused on cooperating simply to survive. Settlers in remote Puritan outposts could not risk further division by blaming members of their own community for doing "the devil's work." This is the main reason no witch trials occurred for nearly half a century.

Generally, one or two decades passed before people felt comfortable enough to confront tensions within their communities. They remained united against such outside threats as the hostile climate, attacks from Native Americans, and epidemic diseases. But as time went on, these events created great fear and suspicion within the remote settlements. Increasingly, the Puritans began to question who among them might be the devil in disguise. Any conflict carried with it the suggestion that some local person was in a pact with the devil and was ultimately responsible for the community's problems. According to the Puritan view of the world, upright Christians had to find ways to eliminate these demonic forces in order to establish the Kingdom of God. As both a sin against God and a crime against the community, witchcraft was therefore punishable by death.

The trials begin

Records of seventeenth-century witch trials are varied in length and detail. All cases that reached the local court systems were documented, while other cases have disappeared into the abyss of forgotten history. Nevertheless, modern historians have been able to gather enough information to reconstruct a fairly accurate picture of the proceedings. In the mid 1600s, prior to the Salem trials, there were ninety-three cases of formal accusations of witchcraft—fifty in Massachusetts and forty-three in Connecticut. A total of sixteen people were put to death, while others were either acquitted (freed from charges) or escaped before they could be executed.

Trials typically started when local authorities received a simple complaint from a "victim" of witchcraft against a suspected "witch." Complaints might range from being bothered by an apparition (spirit or ghost), to falling ill, losing crops, witnessing an act by a malevolent (evil) "spirit," or any number of other disruptions. The suspect would immediately be jailed, then specially appointed officials would begin gathering evidence from townspeople, and sometimes even from the suspect's former neighbors in another village. Usually the officials turned over the evidence to higher courts for hearings. Indictments (pronounced in-DITE-ments; formal accusations) were made by a grand jury, while the verdict (final judgment) was the responsibility of a special trial jury. Final sentencing was determined by court magistrates (civil officers with the power to administer law). Apparently many juries were reluctant to bring convictions, so accused witches were often allowed to provide character witnesses to give positive reports on the person's behavior to aid in their defense. Records also indicate that relatively little torture was used to obtain information from the accused—although it is impossible to know for sure what happened behind locked doors.

There were three typical outcomes to a witch trial: the accused was acquitted (declared innocent) and returned to "normal life" within the community; fled to a different region; or was convicted and executed. Records show that most often people were acquitted of the charges against them. Some lost everything they owned, however, simply because an accusing finger had been pointed at them. Although no general profile fits all cases, an accused witch was usually a middle-aged female living on her own with few or no children. Often the targeted woman was known for her rebellious or disruptive behavior, or she had a reputation as a troublemaker because she went against the grain of the community by, for example, refusing to attend church. Many accused persons were also involved with medicine and the healing arts in some capacity, a position considered fearsome and powerful during these times. A minor record for slander (damaging a person's reputation by making false charges) or petty (minor) theft also helped accusers build a case against a suspect. Not surprisingly, only about 20 percent of accused witches were male, and most of them were considered guilty simply because of their association with suspected witches who were women.

Stories and case studies

The picture of witchcraft in the colonial period is as complex and varied as the imaginations of the people who lived during that time. Witchcraft was a real and frightening

force to the colonists, partly because people believed in its power to harm them and also because it served as a binding force in troubled communities. Case studies and historical data help tell the stories of the victims of these fears. Some stories reveal injustice and prejudice, and others indicate that some people actually believed they were practicing witchcraft. Evidence shows that victims of "witchcraft" were mysteriously changed in inexplicable (unexplainable) physical and psychological (mental) ways. Many communities were quick to judge and try their own people, while others remained skeptical and cautious about falsely accusing innocent people.

The first witch in the New World

The first recorded witch trial in New England resulted in the hanging death of Alse Young in 1647 in Wethersfield, the oldest Puritan settlement in Connecticut. Historians know nothing of the accusations that sent Young to the gallows. Records show, however, that Wethersfield inhabitants had experienced much turmoil in the preceding decade, and at the time Young was executed the community had been struck by a massive, deadly flu and smallpox epidemic. Within a year Mary Johnson of the same town was also hanged as a witch upon her own confession that she had a relationship with the Devil. Johnson was a young, lower-class maidservant who claimed the devil had promised her power and relief from unhappiness if she made a pact with him. It is not known whether she was forced to make this confession to the authorities or she was emotionally unstable, but certainly her case opened a doorway to other trials.

Hard times bring a flurry of trials

In 1648 Margaret Jones was tried and hanged in Charlestown, a village in the Massachusetts Bay Colony. The detailed journals of Governor John Winthrop (1588–1649), which describe the trial and the accusations that led up to it, provide a glimpse into the prevailing superstitions of the day. Jones was an elderly healer and midwife (who assisted in the birthing of babies) in Charlestown. She lived alone and survived on her trade, but she had a history of theft that tainted her reputation and made her a suspect. Her ability to heal was also considered evidence against her, regardless of the outcome of her actions. Patients claimed to fall into violent fits of illness after Jones treated them, and some even became temporarily deaf or blind. Others were miraculously healed, but they charged that her knowledge was supernatural and therefore suspicious. In other words, Jones was doomed by any action she took as a healer, whether she cured or injured her patients, because she was suspected of working for the devil. She was imprisoned and brought to trial as a witch, but she confessed only to committing an act of theft several years earlier. She steadfastly protested accusations of witchcraft. When Puritan authorities examined her body they found a "witch's teat" (an extra nipple). While Jones was being held in jail, witnesses came forward and testified that she had caused the deaths of many local children and that she was often seen with a child spirit that she nursed with her extra teat. This was considered sufficient evidence, and Jones was hanged as a witch.

Anne Hibbens (also spelled Hibbins) of Boston, Massachusetts, was another unfortunate victim of slander and suspicion. Hibbens, the reputedly quarrelsome sister of Governor Bellingham, was widowed in 1654. Thus she was left without the protection of marriage and her former social status. Hibbens was always considered to be cranky and outspoken, but after her husband's death she was directly accused of witchcraft by two women who were her neighbors. The women claimed that while they were talking about Hibbens one day, she came along and confronted them. They testified in court that she had perfectly reconstructed their conversation and then walked away, uttering curses at them. Both women said they suffered minor misfortunes as a result of her curses. Hibbens's case was initially refused by court magistrates, who felt there was not enough evidence to convict her. Nevertheless, other villagers came forward to insist on her guilt, taking the case to the General Court. Hibbens was finally found guilty and executed by hanging in 1656. Even her contemporaries were slightly shocked by the severity of the trial. For instance, the case was later openly condemned by John Norton, a Boston minister, who reportedly said that Hibbens was hanged just for being smarter than her neighbors.

Some cases occurred spontaneously when people suddenly underwent sudden changes in behavior. For example, in 1671 Elizabeth Knapp of Groton, Massachusetts, began experiencing strange symptoms while sitting by her fire one quiet evening. She reported that her throat was closing up and that her breasts, legs, and arms were being pinched hard by invisible forces. She then went into violent convulsions (spasms), leapings, and other strange agitations that came and went for several months. Detailed records of Knapp's case note that during these fits her tongue would be drawn into a semicircle at the roof of her mouth. Often her tongue could not be budged, while other times it would become very long and stiff and protrude from her mouth. Knapp also had hallucinations (imagined visions) about demons, dogs, and witches torturing her and attempting to lead her into satanic activities. While under the influence of these demons, she would speak in strange voices and accuse local people of witchcraft, picking specific individuals out of a crowd with her eyes closed. Yet the Groton community responded to Knapp with surprising restraint. Not a single person—including Knapp—was brought to trial or put to death. Groton residents believed that perhaps the devil was trying to create strife and break down their community by tricking people into turning on each other. This showed that people were

Possession and Hysterics: Modern Psychological Interpretations

Modern psychoanalysts who study abnormal mental conditions have proven that many of the symptoms shown by victims of "witchcraft" can be observed in individuals experiencing severe hysteria, a classified psychological disorder. The sensation of one's throat closing up, for example, is today known as Bolus Hystericus, a common symptom in panic attacks and more advanced stages of hysteria. The disorder makes people feel like they can no longer breathe because of a ball in the throat or "invisible hands" around the neck. Modern psychoanalysts have seen hundreds of patients who have the sensation of being pinched, lapse into convulsive fits, and experience protracted stiffness of the tongue during seizures. Jean Martin Charcot (1825–1893), the nineteenth-century French neurologist, recorded symptoms that exactly match those experienced by victims of "witchcraft." It is especially typical for a hysterical patient to have hallucinations of being persecuted by figures that represent the most dreaded fears. An hysterical patient also becomes paranoid (suspicious) and acts out strong resistance to such encounters. Also common are vivid, imaginary sexual experiences. Victims of hysteria lapse into an extreme psychological state in order to express the dark corners of the psyche.

Psychoanalysts have noted that hysterical fits occur most often in cultures in which people accept these acts as manifestations (displays) of supernatural forces. In seventeenth-century New England fits were a natural extension of the intense fear of evil and God within the extremely strict Puritan society. In other words, by accepting this behavior as real, people were able to explain and deal with one of the most fearsome elements of their culture.

not always ready to surrender to fear and hurl accusations, despite their strong belief that evil was operating among them.

Children possessed by demons

Another case of disturbing psychological symptoms involved four children—three girls and a boy—of John Goodwin, a pious and respected resident of Boston, in 1688. They captured the attention of the minister Cotton Mather, who kept detailed records of his examinations and observations in *The Wonders of the Invisible World* (see the primary sources entry). All four children experienced epileptic fits and convulsions during which they apparently saw demons, rode on horseback, spoke in strange languages, lost the capacity to see or hear, and lashed out at invisible enemies. These activities began when one child got into an argument with Goodwife Glover, their housekeeper, who was immediately suspected of witchcraft. ("Goodwife" was the title Puritans gave to married women.) An interesting aspect of this case is that Glover openly confessed to being a witch and "proved" her own guilt by showing witnesses a collection of fetish dolls she had made. These dolls were small rag puppets stuffed with goat hair (associated with the devil since medieval times) and other significant ingredients. Records show that Glover would utter curses at her victims while rubbing spittle, which was thought to contain magical properties, onto the fetish dolls. When she was brought to court for trial she stroked several of her dolls, causing epileptic seizures and fits in all four children. Upon being asked to provide character witnesses in her own defense, Glover responded that Satan would be her only witness. She was given an immediate death sentence. On the way to the gallows Glover privately told Mather the names of several other "witches." Mather declined to reveal their identities, however, because he felt Glover may have made false accusations in an effort to destroy the community.

After Glover's execution the Goodwin children continued to have fits and seizures, prompting further inquiry into the source of their suffering. Mather decided to take the eldest daughter into his home for several months of observation and prayer. As usual, he kept detailed records of her symptoms. According to his notes, when the girl had fits her belly literally swelled up like a drum. During a fit she also acted like she was conversing with demons while riding on a wildly galloping horse. Even when she was in a quiet state she was unable to utter certain words like "God" and "Jesus" while praying. (This symptom has since been found in studies of hysterical patients.) Eventually all four children were "prayed" out of their fits and they lived to ripe old ages, never once discrediting their experiences. Mather, for his part, regarded the Goodwin case as proof of witchcraft in the colonies and used it to warn other communities. Although he told people to remain skeptical of accusations, he simply succeeded in spreading belief in witchcraft. Many people were acquitted in court because communities feared they were being tricked by the devil into killing innocent people. Yet cases like the Goodwin children's "bewitchment" only served as fuel for the fire.

Katherine Harrison: The Typical Witch

Katherine Harrison of Wethersfield, Connecticut, was a healer who was widowed in 1666. A capable healer, she had a reputation for incredible physical strength, had inherited a fortune, and never went to church. All these factors made her a prime candidate for suspicion of witchcraft. Like many New England communities, Wethersfield had experienced intense stress and conflict. Between 1665 and 1667 the town was struck by a devastating smallpox epidemic, massive drought, blight, a ruined crop season, economic setbacks, conflicts with Quakers (people who follow the religion Society of Friends), and skirmishes with Native Americans. Not surprisingly, Harrison was accused of being a witch shortly after these events had come to an end. Her case was typical in that many people testified against her, including members of a community where she had lived previously. Most of the testimonials revealed that she caused severe illnesses and deaths and frightened people by appearing in different shapes and forms. Brought to trial in 1668, Harrison was acquitted (freed of the charges) in court the following year. Nevertheless, she was forced to leave Wethersfield, and her reputation followed her when she moved to Westchester, New York. Fearing her powers, villagers demanded that she leave. She went to the local courts to argue for her right to live in Westchester and won.

Bad weather, locusts, and witches

Historians have studied other events that took place in New England during the 1600s and have found remarkable ties between community stress and accusations of witchcraft. During times of social unrest or tension or during natural disasters there were no cases of witchcraft. Immediately after the conflict or disaster had ended, however, the number of accusations rose. Because the Puritans shunned scientific interpretation of natural events (relying on the Bible instead), they had no way to explain what was happening to and around them. Three types of events in particular led directly to witch trials: epidemics, natural disasters, and extreme weather. Settlers faced enormous problems with epidemics: influenza, smallpox, measles, and dysentery produced massive fatality rates. The same was true of natural disasters, which took the settlers by surprise as they tried to adapt to a new environment. They were almost totally dependent on favorable weather for survival, so drought, flooding, hurricanes, or hard winters could destroy entire communities. These phenomena are listed in diaries and other records, again showing a link between natural disasters and accusations of witchcraft.

A community that happened to survive a harsh winter or an epidemic still had to contend with other dangers. Blight and pestilence (crop diseases, fungus, and insects) were a major challenge to good harvests. In 1663, for instance, an enormous blight epidemic started in Massachusetts and spread throughout the Northeast. In addition to destroying an entire season of wheat, it terrified the settlers. Caterpillars and tiny crop-eating flies also caused significant damage, wiping out whole orchards and entire fields of barley, oats, and corn. In this era fires could be especially devastating, leveling neighborhoods within days and setting back years of hard work. Boston seems to have been especially vulnerable, with at least five major fires breaking out between 1643 and 1692 and destroying more than half of the city each time. The Puritans interpreted all these events as punishment for sin or as a challenge from the devil.

Puritans were frightened by other natural events, which they read as further signs of evil. They linked comets, eclipses, auroras (streamers of light in the sky), and earthquakes with ruined crops or the death of a local leader. Even rainbows were viewed as God shooting at somebody. Community members were often blamed for such occurrences and charged with witchcraft. If a person died after an eclipse, for example, the Puritans believed that someone was exerting a supernatural evil force. In 1692 Salem, Massachusetts, had just recovered from war, epidemic, and political upheaval. Thus the community was ripe for a massive explosion of hysteria, panic, and accusation.

For Further Study

Demos, John Putnam. *Entertaining Satan: Witchcraft and the Culture of Early New England.* New York: Oxford University Press, 1982.

Elliot, Emory, ed. *American Literature: A Prentice Hall Anthology,* Volume 1. New York: Prentice Hall, 1991.

Stern, Wendy. *Witches: Opposing viewpoints.* San Diego, California: Greenhaven Press, 1995.

Salem Town and Salem Village

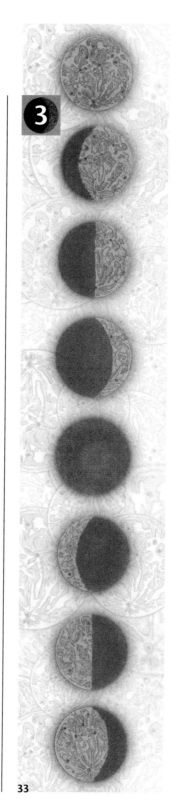

3

In early 1692 Salem, Massachusetts, was in a period of transition. The community was recovering from fifteen brutal years of regional conflict and disaster that had produced deep local tensions. During this time New Englanders had experienced severe epidemics, warfare with Native Americans, and high mortality (death) rates. They also suffered a major constitutional setback: in 1684 England revoked the charters (government deeds) of the New England colonies, taking away the colonies' form of self rule. Four years later a British official, Sir Edmund Andros (1637–1714), was appointed as governor. This act effectively nullified (made void; ended) all former land titles, taking away legal claims to some properties and plunging the region into chaos. Angry colonists rebelled and overthrew Andros's government. The Massachusetts charter was restored in 1691, uniting the Massachusetts Bay Colony with Plymouth and Maine. Yet the political struggle had put great stress on the Puritans. Not only had they fought among themselves over land rights, they were also convinced that God was unhappy with them and would perhaps bring other punishments upon them. During the Salem trials in 1693, Boston minister **Cotton Mather** (see biography and primary sources entries) described the situation:

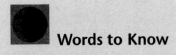

Words to Know

acute: severe

apparition: ghostly figure

calamity: disaster

culprit: person or thing responsible for something, usually bad

disobedient: not obeying the rules

frail: fragile

hamlet: small village

indentured servant: one who signs a contract to work for an employer for a specified length of time

magistrate: an official of the courts

I believe there never was a poor plantation more pursued . . . than our New England. First, the Indian Powwows . . . then seducing spirits . . . after this a continual blast upon some of our principal grains . . . . Herewithal, wasting sickness. . . . Next, so many adversaries of our own language . . . desolating fires also . . . and losses by sea. . . . Besides all which, the devils are come upon us with such wrath as is justly . . . the astonishment of the world. (From John Putnam Demos, *Entertaining Satan*, p. 313.)

Salem Town against Salem Village

During this time Salem was beset by internal conflicts that became crucial to the later witch trials. The six hundred Salem residents lived in two distinctly different communities—Salem Town and Salem Village. The town was located closer to the Atlantic coast and had become a bustling, urban commercial center with many affluent citizens. In contrast, the village was an isolated agricultural hamlet of a few scattered houses and farms. In the winter residents had to walk up to two hours just to go from one side of the village to the other because of the wilderness and harsh weather conditions. Salem villagers were mostly farmers and servants who adhered to more traditional religious and social values than town residents. Community relations were further strained as the town underwent an economic boom and the village remained a struggling settlement. By the early 1690s a marked class division had developed between the town and the village. Discord reached a peak as Salem residents argued about land rights and economic problems. Several other issues contributed to mounting tensions. For instance, Salem leaders argued about when and how men should pass down their property, often setting father against son. They were also trying to determine whether power and authority should stay in the hands of the established elite, or whether the merchant class could become part of the ruling group. Still another struggle involved deciding how much political power should be shared between the upper and lower classes.

Although Salem Town had political and religious authority over Salem Village, about half of the villagers felt they should rule themselves. Preacher **Samuel Parris** (see biography entry), a newcomer to the area, was the controversial leader of a group that wanted independence from Salem Town. The villagers who favored self-rule gathered around Parris and his close friends, the Putnams, who owned most of the farming land in Salem Village. In fact, witchcraft accusations started in the Parris household, and many of the accusers were villagers. Targets of the accusations lived in Salem Town or were villagers who did not support the separation movement. Tensions ran so deep that in 1692 Salem was basically dry kindling waiting for a spark to ignite it.

Sir Edmund Andros was sent from Great Britain to act as the governor of the New England colonies. *Reproduced by permission of Archive Photos, Inc.*

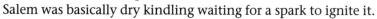

Parris controversy fuels trials

Samuel Parris was born in London, England, and made his first attempt at a career as a sugar merchant in Barbados, an island in the West Indies in the Caribbean. When a hurricane wrecked his business he moved to Boston, Massachussetts, with his family and tried to start over. After failing again as a merchant, Parris decided to become a minister. He moved to Salem Village in 1688, bringing with him his wife, three children, a niece, and two slaves. He was hired by the Putnam family to take over the congregation—which consisted mainly of the Putnams and their relatives—that was separate from the one in town. Normally, a town minister would receive a modest salary, the use of a house, and free firewood as payment for his services. Parris got all of these benefits in addition to the title and deed to the parish (the

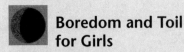

Boredom and Toil for Girls

In New England winter was a time of relaxation for men and boys, who traditionally farmed and worked outdoors in the summertime. They spent the long, bitterly cold days socializing, hunting and fishing, and visiting their neighbors. Yet there was no rest for women, who continued the monotonous and difficult household chores that sustained their families through the season. Young girls helped their mothers with sewing, spinning, washing, and cooking. Play was a forbidden activity for children, and they were faced with long boring months of isolation and hard work inside as winter raged outside. Boredom and unrelenting work for girls became a major factor in the Salem trials.

area where the congregation members live) that surrounded his land. This deal angered residents who did not want separate churches for the village and the town. They saw Parris as an unnecessary drain on meager resources. They rebelled by not paying their local taxes, which paid Parris's salary, and refusing to worship at the Salem Village meetinghouse. In 1691 they elected a committee, made up mostly of Parris opponents, who ruled against using taxes for his salary and revoked the deed to his house and land. As a result, Parris would have to sustain himself and his family solely off voluntary contributions. Nevertheless, lines had been drawn between the powerful Putnams on one side and opponents of Parris on the other. Events were set in motion for the Salem trials that came later the next year.

Winter 1691–92 in the Parris home

Tales of voodoo by the fire

During the winter of 1691–92 the Parris household became the center of witchcraft accusations. Living in the home were Parris's nine-year-old daughter Elizabeth (called Betty), his eleven-year-old niece Abigail Williams, and two other children. Betty was a quiet, obedient child known for her deep fear of the devil, which no doubt came from hearing her father's fiery sermons. Abigail, on the other hand, was a bolder, more impulsive girl who felt protected by her connection to God through her uncle. Also living in the house were the Parrises' two slaves— **Tituba** (see biography entry), an older Caribbean woman (half African, half Carrib Indian), and her husband, John Indian, a Carrib Indian. Tituba took care of the girls and did most of the indoor chores, while John Indian helped Samuel Parris with outdoor tasks. Tituba, Betty, and Abigail spent most of the time cooped up

Salem Village in the
seventeenth century
was a small but
busy settlement.
*Reproduced by permission
of the Corbis Corporation
(Bellevue).*

inside doing chores together. All three escaped the boredom of
their daily lives by taking short breaks when Parris and his wife
were out socializing with other parishioners. To pass the time
Tituba and the girls would sit by the fireplace and tell stories.
Tituba captured the girls' imaginations with fantastic tales of
voodoo (a form of magic) tricks, spells, and charms she learned
while growing up in Barbados. Although the Parrises had forbidden Betty and Abigail to discuss voodoo, they encouraged
Tituba's stories and savored the often frightening details.

Fear and Tituba's circle

As the storytelling sessions became more intense, Betty
and Abigail—both God-fearing Puritans—began to worry that
they were committing evil. In this era even children were
made to feel the heavy weight of obedience and sin. From an
early age they had heard sermons that were meant to inspire
fear in adults as well as children. An excerpt from another of

Mather's books, *The Good Education of Children,* 1708, is typical of the messages aimed at the minds of young Puritans:

> Do you dare to run up and down on the Lord's day? Or do you keep in to read your book? They which lie must go to their father the devil, into an everlasting burning; they which never pray, God will pour out his wrath upon them; and when they beg and pray in hellfire, God will not forgive them, but there they must lie forever. Are you willing to go to Hell to be burnt with the devil and his angels? Oh the Hell is a terrible place, that's worse a thousand times than whipping. (From Earle Rice, Jr. *The Salem Witch Trials.* p. 23.)

Not only were Betty and Abigail under intense pressure from their Puritan faith, they also had to endure the burden of living in Samuel Parris's household. They were surely aware of the controversy about his status in the community, and they must have known that the family would become poverty-stricken if Parris lost his income. The pleasure they took in Tituba's stories also gave them a sense of doom, which they felt powerless to fight. Fear and fascination led the girls to confide in a few friends, who too began attending the storytelling sessions. Tituba's new listeners included **Ann Putnam, Jr.** (see biography and primary source entries), the twelve-year-old daughter of Parris's main supporters. Other girls in the group were Mary Walcott, the sixteen-year-old daughter of Captain Jonathan Walcott; Elizabeth Hubbard, the seventeen-year-old great-niece of the village physician, William Griggs; Susan Sheldon; and Elizabeth Booth. Also coming to the Parris fireside were nineteen-year-old Mercy Lewis, who lived with the Putnams, and Mary Warren, a twenty-year-old servant in the village tavern run by **John Proctor** (see biography entry).

The beginning of the crisis

The coffin and the egg

On January 20, 1692, the girls were experimenting with one of Tituba's voodoo fortune-telling tricks. They dropped an egg white into a glass of warm water, then waited for the egg to turn into the face of the man a certain girl would marry. But when Betty looked into the glass she saw the shape of a coffin instead of a man's face. She immediately flew into hysterics. She started ranting and raving, at times crouching on her hands and knees and barking like a dog. She also had severe convulsions (spasms) and seizures. Betty's symptoms were so extreme that ripples of fear spread quickly throughout the village: the devil was afoot and threatening to destroy Salem from within the very heart of their religious community.

Betty never recovered from her sickness and other girls, including Abigail, fell ill with similar symptoms. Within several weeks suspicions of witchcraft turned into accusations. Parris wrote in his diary, quoted in *Entertaining Satan,* that "When these calamities first began, which was in my own family, the affliction was several weeks before such hellish operations as witchcraft were suspected." Dr. Griggs examined the girls in early February, when it became clear that the afflictions were not going away. He announced that the girls were physically healthy but were "under an evil hand," thus making the first formal claim of witchcraft as the culprit in this bizarre behavior. News of the girls' "bewitchment" quickly spread through the region. The panic was heightened by the recent publication of Mather's 1693 book *Wonders of the Invisible World,* which reported his observations of the Goodwin children in Boston (see Chapter 2). The symptoms were similar enough to make people believe that the same fate was being visited upon Salem.

On February 25, 1692, Mary Sibley, the aunt of one of the afflicted girls, enlisted the help of Tituba and John Indian in determining whether witchcraft was at play in Salem Village. She ordered them to bake a "witch's cake" consisting of a batter mixed with Betty and Abigail's urine. The cake was to be fed to the Parrises' dog, which would prove a witch's spell if he turned into a "familiar," an animal inhabited by the spirit of a

Many Puritans had visions of witches standing over cauldrons, mixing up potions and casting spells. *Reproduced by permission of Archive Photos, Inc.*

Possible Culprit in Salem: The Ergot Fungus

Contemporary scientists may have found a new culprit in the Salem witchcraft trials: ergot (Claviceps purpurea), a fungus that grows on rye wheat. This fungus can withstand freezing temperatures and may be taken into the body either through contaminated wheat in bread or in milk from cows grazing in contaminated fields. In small doses ergot can cause muscle contractions that result in such symptoms as spontaneous abortion and minor damage to the central nervous system. In large doses it can cause ergotism, a condition in humans characterized by disorientation (not knowing who or where you are), hallucination (imagined visions), muscle cramps, convulsions (spasms), seizures, vomiting, and even a deadly form of gangrene (rotting of the flesh). Since the Salem trials, more specific symptoms have been recorded during outbreaks of the fungus. Among them are depression, psychosis (mental derangement), delirium (confusion), a crawling sensation on the skin, and a sense of being pinched all over the body. LSD (lysergic acid diethylamide), a drug known for its hallucinatory effects, is chemically related to the ergot fungus.

Scientists began investigating ergot in 1951, when the fungus contaminated wheat used for making bread in a small town in France. Almost all the affected villagers claimed to feel burning sensations in their limbs, had hallucinations that they could fly, and were gripped by other symptoms. These reactions have led some scientists and historians to speculate on the witch trials in New England. It is possible that the Puritans' belief in witches, the stresses of frontier living, and outbreaks of ergotism converged to create a crisis. It would help explain how people may have genuinely believed that witchcraft had caused their suffering. Perhaps a small fungus changed the course of history for an entire population.

witch. No record remains of the dog's reaction. It is known, however, that Parris found out about the witch's cake and became infuriated by attempts to use witchcraft in his own home. He publicly denounced Sibley for getting the devil's attention, thus playing on the fear that evil was breaking loose into the village through prominent people. Sibley confessed to the crime of using witchcraft, and perhaps the girls realized they could deflect some of the blame onto others. Terrified that their own "crimes"—such as mixing the egg-white potion—would be discovered, the girls began pointing fingers.

The first three Salem "witches"

Tituba, Sarah Good, and Sarah Osborne

On February 29, 1692, Salem villagers Thomas and Edward Putnam, Joseph Hutchinson, and Thomas Preston together swore official complaints in court against Tituba, Sarah Good, and Sarah Osborne. These men were all supporters of Samuel Parris, who said that Betty and Abigail had identified the women as witches. Besides Tituba, thirty-nine-year-old Sarah Good was the first person to be accused. According to *The Salem Witch Trials* Ann Putnam, Jr. swore to Magistrates John Hathorne and Johnathan Corwin that she been plagued by an "apparition of Sarah Good which did torture [her] most grievously." She claimed the apparition then pinched and pricked her for days, while urging her to become a witch. Putnam also said she had witnessed Good doing the same things to other girls, who all confirmed her charges for the magistrates. The three accused witches were taken to jail on March 1 and exam-

Once the witchcraft hysteria started no one was safe from being accused.
Reproduced by permission of the Corbis Corporation (Bellevue).

ined for marks by the magistrates. On this fateful day, Tituba readily confessed to the crime of witchcraft and proclaimed the guilt of Good and Osborne as well. Perhaps she thought she stood a better chance of being released if she admitted to a relationship with Satan and accused the other women of evil acts.

Sarah Good's unlucky past

Sarah Good was pregnant, widowed, and poor, with a four-year-old child at the time charges of witchcraft were brought against her. She had had an extremely difficult life. In 1672, when she was a teenager, her father, John Solart, committed suicide and brought scorn and suspicion on his family. The Solarts were living in nearby Wendham village, and they were one of many families involved in disputes over land rights that had caused divisions between Salem Town and Salem Village. Solart's widow remarried, but she refused to share most of his estate with their seven children, leaving them to fend for themselves. Sarah managed to get a few acres of her mother's property near Salem Village, then married Daniel Poole, an indentured servant (one who signs a contract to work for an employer for a specified length of time). Poole died almost immediately, leaving Sarah deeply in debt. When she married William Good, Poole's creditors seized their land as payment for Poole's debts. Now homeless, the Goods begged for food and shelter. Sarah also began to age beyond her years because her life had been so stressful: village records reveal that when she was in her late thirties she appeared to be around seventy years old. Sarah Good's present circumstances and family history made her a prime candidate for accusations of witchcraft. Once she was charged, she could not refute the "spectral evidence"—proof of association with evil spirits—that was the primary weapon against her. Court records show that the magistrates bullied Good and accepted accusations made by Betty Parris and Abigail Williams, even though there was a lack of physical evidence.

Sarah Osborne falls prey to suspicion

When Sarah Good was first examined by the magistrates, she denied the charges against her. Moreover, she announced that Sarah Osborne was responsible for the fits experienced by Betty and Abigail, thus confirming the girls'

The Psychology of Fear and Punishment

Modern psychologists who study the mind and behavior have classified the experiences of the girls in the Parris household as typical hysteria, more specifically a condition called conversion reaction. This condition occurs in situations in which the victim is terrified of being discovered and punished for some crime, usually imagined. Common in children who have been severely beaten or sexually abused, conversion reaction reflects both an individual experience and a response to the psychological environment of an entire community. In the Parris case, the girls most likely became immersed in the drama of Tituba's stories while feeling ashamed and frightened about being disobedient. They must have been frightened of the "evil" they had conjured up, and were terrified of what Reverend Parris might do to them if he found out they had "invited" trouble into his home. The fear they experienced the day they saw the image of a coffin in water would have certainly been enough to put them into a state of deep hysteria.

Indeed, the girls went through the typical stages of hysteria, starting with a preliminary phase of anxious self-reflection or worrying about their "sins." At this point they realized that they were endangering their own spiritual condition and possibly angering God. This led to the onset phase, which is characterized by fainting, wailing, and broken speech. These symptoms intensified when people became alarmed at the strange behavior of the girls, who then began to have visions of witches. Next was the acute phase, during which the girls experienced intense physical sensations. For instance, they felt like they were burning or being pinched by demons. They also thought they could fly, contorted themselves into strange positions, and acted out interactions with witches. A final stage, known as intermission, punctuated the acute phase with moments of calm or deep depression that came and went for hours or days at a time.

accusations. Osborne was a frail sixty-nine-year-old invalid who also came under suspicion because of land disputes. Her first husband, Robert Prince, had been a successful and active citizen who owned over 150 acres of land along a controversial dividing line between Salem Village and the adjacent (next) town of Topsfield. When Prince died, Sarah married their indentured servant John Osborne and tried to change the terms of her dead husband's will. Prince had specified that his two sons, who were only two and six years old at the time of his death, should take over the land when they became adults. He had appointed Thomas and John Putnam, his in-laws, to supervise the trust. Sarah's attempt to change the will put her in direct opposition to the powerful Putnams and raised suspicions about her character. To make matters worse, neither Sarah Good nor Sarah Osborne attended the Salem Village church. Tituba and the two Sarahs were presumed guilty prior to any formal court hearing. They were sent to a Boston jail on March 7, 1692, to await the beginning of the first official Salem trials.

For Further Study

Demos, John Putnam. *Entertaining Satan.* Oxford: Oxford University Press, 1982.

Discovery Online—A Village Possessed: A True Story of Witchcraft. [Online] http://www.discovery.com/stories/history/witches/witches.html (Accessed July 7, 2000).

Hill, Frances. *A Delusion of Satan: The Full Story of the Salem Witch Trials.* New York: Doubleday, 1995.

Rice, Earle, Jr. *The Salem Witch Trials.* San Diego, California: Lucent Books, 1997.

The Salem Witch Museum. [Online] http://www.salemwitchmuseum.com/ (Accessed July 7, 2000).

Salem Witch Trials and Executions

4

The pre-trial hearings in the cases of Sarah Good, Sarah Osborne, and Tituba set the stage for the social strife that would soon rip Salem apart. (See Chapter 3 for information on the circumstances that led to the arrests of these three women on witchcraft charges; also see Tituba's biography entry.) At first no one suspected that Tituba, Elizabeth (Betty) Parris, Abigail Williams, and the other young girls could be lying. After all there was "damning evidence": Tituba had confessed to practicing witchcraft, and the girls had clearly been bewitched by Good, Osborne, and Tituba. During the hearing on March 1, 1692, both Good and Osborne denied the charges against them, pleading for justice and fairness. Yet, according to court records, chief magistrate (judge) John Hathorne deliberately invited several girls to identify Osborne as a witch, telling "all the children to stand up and look upon her [Osborne] and see if they did know her which they all did and every one of them said that this was one of the women that did afflict them and that they had constantly seen her in the very habit [clothing] that she was now in."

The accusing girls were immediately seized by such severe fits that their mouths bled and their tongues became stiff.

Words to Know

amnesty: pardon

devastation: physically or mentally destroyed

elicit: to draw out

embellish: add to in an exaggerated way

gruesome: disgusting

jeer: making fun of

jurisdiction: area of legal coverage, as in a court system

pardon: excuse

rebuked: strongly criticized

reign: rule

reprieve: pardon

rivalry: competition

specter: ghostly figure

strife: suffering

In desperation, Osborne at first pleaded innocent; she then shifted tactics, claiming, as quoted by Rice, she had been haunted by "an Indian, all black, which did pinch her in her neck." She went on to imply that Tituba had haunted her for several months, repeatedly ordering her to stop attending church. Osborne thus sealed her own fate by focusing attention on the fact that she frequently missed worship services. When the court asked Osborne's husband and neighbors if she had been to church on Sundays in the past few months, they admitted that she was often absent. In attempting to deflect attention onto Tituba, Osborne inadvertently (accidentally) made herself look like a liar and a co-conspirator.

When Tituba was called upon to speak, she not only doomed the two Sarahs but many others as well. Tituba announced that the children had not been bewitched by spirits but instead by the devil himself, who often appeared to her as a tall man carrying a witches' book. According to Tituba, the book contained the names of nine local witches, two of them being Osborne and Good. Tituba's confession was perhaps even more dramatic than the children's fits, for it fed the worst fears of the crowd in the courtroom. She exaggerated her story with fantastic descriptions of riding to Sabbath (mass meeting of witches) with both Sarahs on a broomstick, at which point the girls again began thrashing about in fits. Tituba herself went into a fit and claimed to have become blind, confirming a popular superstition that when a witch gives up her power she loses her sight.

The monster of Salem

When Tituba, Osborne, and Good were put in jail to await formal trial, Salem residents set about eradicating other

As Elizabeth Proctor tried to reason with the courts, the "afflicted" girls screamed, moaned, and convulsed.
Reproduced by permission of North Wind Pictures Archive.

witches from their midst. At this point fear and politics merged to become the monster of Salem. Under the influence of their politically motivated relatives, the girls began pointing fingers at more people, some of whom were highly regarded members of the community. The first such victim was Elizabeth Proctor, wife of tavern owner **John Proctor** (see biography entry). She publicly questioned the validity of the girls' fits, suggesting that there was more to the hearings than simple accusations of witchcraft. Elizabeth was more outspoken than her husband, but he supported her right to express her doubts, thus bringing himself under suspicion. Although the Proctors were not involved in local land disputes, they posed a threat to the Putnams, a family who wielded considerable power in Salem Village (see Chapter 3). The main accusers of witches were Ann Putnam, Sr. and **Ann Putnam, Jr.** (see biography and primary source entries), wife and daughter, respectively, of Salem Village leader Thomas Putnam. Joseph Putnam, Thomas's own brother, reportedly backed Elizabeth Proctor's statements.

According to records, as related by Rice, Joseph went to Thomas's house and warned him not to spread his "foul lies" any further in the family. The Proctors' protests and Joseph Putnam's warning marked the beginning of doubt that soon caused a separation between those who believed the evidence and others who dared to resist the hysteria. Such vocal opponents as the Proctors and Putnam managed to keep some people from joining in the frenzy, but their efforts were not enough to stop the tide of accusations.

A day of prayer in Salem Village

In early March, Betty Parris was sent to live at the home of Stephen Sewall, a court clerk, in Salem Town in order to give her some distance from the trials. She evidently stopped having fits and was restored to her more stable nature. The other girls were never formally separated from one other, however, and continued to meet whenever possible. Each rendezvous resulted in another series of accusations. On March 11 the village of Salem held a day of fasting (the act of abstaining from food or drink) and prayer to contemplate the presence of witchcraft in their community. The event was a genuine attempt by villagers to seek spiritual guidance and to examine their own roles in the charges against their fellow citizens. It could have been a turning point away from hysteria had the girls not been present at the service: once again they took center stage with their convulsions. This time they shocked the entire community by pointing the finger at an unlikely candidate, the highly respected and elderly Martha Corey.

Attacking Martha Corey

Martha Corey (also spelled Cory) was eighty-one years old and the third wife of Giles Corey, a wealthy landowner whose property straddled the line between Salem Village and Salem Town. Though a faithful church member, she was known for being opinionated. She had also created a ripple of controversy early in her adult life by giving birth to an illegitimate mulatto (of mixed racial descent) child. These factors combined against Martha Corey when, on March 19, Edward Putnam, a member of the powerful Putnam family, and Ezekiel Cheever, the court reporter, came to her home and accused her of practicing witchcraft. Prior to their visit Corey's primary accuser, Ann Putnam, Jr, claimed that she had been temporarily blinded and could not describe the clothing Corey was wearing when the old woman had supposedly bewitched her. Edward Putnam and Cheever confronted Corey with evidence that she had afflicted Ann and other girls. Although Corey denied accusations of witchcraft, she tried to outsmart the men by saying, "But does she tell you what I have on?"—implying that Ann might be accusing the wrong person. Corey's accusers took this statement as a sign that she not only knew they could not answer the question but she was also playing a trick on them—that she was, in fact, a witch. Edward Putnam and Cheever immediately arrested Corey on charges of committing injuries against Ann and other girls—Mercy Lewis, Elizabeth Hubbard, and Abigail Williams. Another "injured" person on the list was Ann Putnam, Sr., who had also testified against Corey and another elderly church member, Rebecca Nurse (see *The Testimony Ann Putnam, Sr. against Martha Corey and Rebecca Nurse* in the primary sources section).

Since the warrant was issued on a Saturday, Corey had one more chance to give her side of the story. Local law made Saturday and Sunday sacred days of prayer on which no person could be arrested. Corey attended church for the last time on Sunday, March 20. During the service a special sermon was delivered by a visiting minister, Deodat Lawson, who had come to town to investigate the situation. Having recently lost his wife and daughter to illness, Lawson was overcome with grief and therefore ready to blame their deaths on witchcraft. He thus devoted his day–long sermon to the need to resist the forces of evil through religious faith. Throughout the day the girls put on a spectacular show of fits and accusations, claiming to see specters (ghostly images) of Corey all over the church in various tormenting poses. At one point, as noted in *A Village Possessed*, Abigail Williams interrupted the sermon by screaming out, "Look where Goodwife Corey sits on the beam suckling [nursing] her yellow bird between her fingers!" Ann Putnam, Jr. then ran up to Lawson and echoed Abigail's accusation. She claimed she saw a yellow bird with Corey's face sitting on Lawson's hat as it hung on the wall in the pulpit.

These antics ruined Corey's opportunity to gain support from her fellow villagers. The event also ushered in another vital aspect of the witch-hunts—spectral evidence—which would eventually ruin the lives of several people. While spectral evidence was not a new phenomenon, it was becoming the main source of proof against people accused of witchcraft. Consequently, anyone could claim to see another person's image committing some foul act. Spectral evidence turned into a powerful weapon that could be used against any member of the community, regardless of status. Thus, since the girls had a monopoly on attention, they could effectively bring down anyone they chose to accuse simply by lapsing into convulsions and conjuring up specters. Even people such as the well-loved and respected Martha Corey could not fight their accusations.

During Corey's court trial on March 21 both spectral evidence and the clothing coincidence were used against her. Corey tried to defend herself by explaining that a friend, who was present in the Putnam home when Ann Putnam, Jr., supposedly went blind, had rushed to tell her about the accusations. Corey said her friend's warning was the reason she had known to ask whether or not Ann could describe her clothing. When the court questioned Corey's friend, however, he denied ever telling her such a thing. Giles Corey also could not recall his wife being visited by the friend, thus reinforcing the conclusion that she was a liar. During the trial the girls reacted to any sign of nervous tension exhibited by Martha Corey. When she wrung her hands or twitched they threw themselves into massive fits, stopping only to exclaim that they saw a man whispering into Corey's ear whenever she was being questioned. Corey was found guilty and sentenced to be hanged, yet she maintained her innocence. (See *The Testimony of Ann Putnam, Sr. against Martha Corey and Rebecca Nurse* in the primary sources section.)

The trial of Rebecca Nurse

After Corey was found guilty accusations began flying anew across Salem Village and taking down other respected people. During Corey's trial, Reverend Lawson paid a visit to the home of Salem Village preacher **Samuel Parris** (see biography entry), where Parris's neice Abigail Williams was living (see Chapter 3). Lawson witnessed Abigail undergoing a particularly severe fit. During the commotion she repeatedly

claimed to see fellow villager Rebecca Nurse standing in front of her and coaxing her to sign the witches' book. Abigail made an elaborate show of refusing to sign the book. She ran to the fireplace and picked up hot embers, which she threw around the room with her bare hands. During the next few days Ann Putnam, Sr., met with the girls at the local tavern. She also began having fits. On March 23 the other girls accused Nurse of practicing witchcraft. This turn of events was even more dramatic than the charges against Corey, for Nurse was a seventy-five-year-old woman renowned throughout the village for her kindness and piety. She was, in other words, a model citizen and one of the least likely candidates for victimization in the witch-hunt craze. Nurse's neighbors Israel and Elizabeth Porter immediately warned her about the charges being brought against her. Responding with typical kindness, Nurse said she was worried about the girls and declared that other accused "witches" were also innocent. The Porters later wrote a formal statement that proclaimed Nurse's innocence, yet it was not enough to protect her.

On March 24, 1692, Edward and Jonathan Putnam (uncle and cousin, respectively, of Ann, Jr.) swore out a formal complaint against Nurse and issued a warrant for her arrest on charges of criminal witchcraft against the entire group of girls. When Nurse was taken to the meetinghouse (the term for a Puritan church) for a pretrial hearing, two factions (opposing groups) immediately formed over the issue of her guilt or innocence. Even Hathorne took a remarkably gentle approach in questioning her, even showing some pity. In the meetinghouse Nurse told the crowd that not only had she been lying in bed gravely ill for the past eighty-nine days, she had never harmed anyone in her entire life. When she was accused of murdering several children, she suggested another possibility, as quoted in Rice's *Salem Witch Trials:* "I do not know what to think of it. . . . The Devil may appear in any shape." Nurse's response suggested a new theory in the minds of some citizens: perhaps the devil was wandering around taking on the images of respectable people in order to trick them into turning against one another. Nurse was sent to jail to await trial.

The tragic month of April

The month of April 1692 ushered in an even greater tide of accusations and trials, each case fueling panic, social strife, and hysteria. By the end of April twenty-three more suspects were targeted in Salem Village, along with several others in neighboring towns. On April 3, Samuel Parris read a sermon in which he condemned both Nurse and Corey, who were members of his own congregation. Stressing the Puritan notion of predestination (that one's fate is already sealed), he suggested that the accused "witches" had been chosen by God, even before birth, to go to Hell, in the Christian concept of eternal punishment after death. Parris went on to say that the worst crime against the church was to serve the devil from within the congregation itself. During the service a parishioner named Sarah Cloyce got up and stormed from the room, slamming the door behind her.

The Towne-Putnam feud

An angry Parris immediately accused Cloyce of being yet another witch spreading evil among the good Christians of

Salem. Her defenders asserted, however, she had taken ill suddenly and that a gust of wind had slammed the door as she left in haste. Historians note that Parris clearly had a political motivation for calling Cloyce a witch: she was the sister of Rebecca Nurse. The women were members of the Towne family, longtime enemies of the powerful Putnam clan, who had started the Salem Village congregation for Parris. The feud between the Townes and the Putnams had begun in 1639, when the Massachusetts General Court gave Salem Village permission to expand in the direction of the Ipswich River. Six years earlier, however, the court had also granted the village of Ipswich permission to expand in the same location. The town of Topsfield, which lay between Salem and Ipswich, became the site of conflict that lasted for several decades. At Topsfield four main families competed for the right to mark boundaries on the land they had all been granted by the government. John Putnam, head of the Putnam family, fought against the Howes, Townes, and Eastys. During a dispute over rights to woodlands, Jacob Towne (the father of Nurse, Cloyce, and Elizabeth Proctor) cut down one of Putnam's trees in full view of Putnam himself. In retaliation Putnam returned with a group of his relatives and threatened to cut down all of Towne's trees. Thus began a feud that continued for over fifty years and culminated in the Salem trials, when the Putnams targeted their Towne rivals in a final show of force.

Sealing fates

After Cloyce left the church the girls became highly agitated and claimed to have a vision of a large group of witches standing by a devil's church, with Cloyce and Sarah Good serving as deacons (church officials). Without hesitation the congregation accepted this vision as proof that members of their own community were working with the devil to destroy them. Cloyce and Proctor (who was pregnant at the time) were arrested shortly thereafter. They appeared in court on April 11 in the first case to be tried in Salem Town. The trials were elevated to celebrity status when six Massachusetts dignitaries traveled from Boston to Salem to serve as judges and observers in the proceedings. Among them were Thomas Danforth, the deputy governor, and court clerk Stephen Sewall's brother

Samuel Sewall, who kept an extensive diary of the trials (see biography and primary source entries). Danforth presided over the trials, showing even less skepticism about the girls' behavior than local residents who had known the girls prior to their fits. His attitude greatly boosted the girls' credibility and spread fear throughout Massachusetts. In a sense Danforth had put a stamp of approval on the girls and determined the outcome of the trials.

During Cloyce's trial Danforth interrogated John Indian (Tituba's husband), Mary Walcott, and Abigail Williams for evidence to be used against Cloyce. John Indian claimed he had been injured by both Proctor and Cloyce when they choked him and tried to force him to sign their witches' book. At this point, according to the court record quoted in *The Salem Witch Trials*, Cloyce stood up in the courtroom and screamed out in anger: "When did I ever hurt you?" John Indian calmly replied, "A great many times." When Abigail was asked about her visions she said she had seen about forty people gathered in a witches' Sabbath, where Cloyce and Good were acting as ministers of the devil. This was sufficient evidence to condemn Cloyce to death.

During Proctor's trial Danforth asked similar questions of the accusers. Yet none of the girls stepped forward to call Proctor a witch, and one of them even said, "I never saw her so as to be hurt by her." Then John Indian claimed that Proctor's specter had attempted to choke him. While the girls remained silent Danforth asked Proctor about John Indian's charge. She replied, "I take God in Heaven to be my witness that I know nothing of it, no more than the child unborn." Suddenly the girls became animated and declared that Proctor had tried to get them to sign the devil's book. In response to this new accusation she calmly maintained her innocence, hinting that the girls would later be judged by God for telling lies. At this point Abigail and Ann Putnam, Jr., went into severe fits, exclaiming that Proctor's specter was taunting them from the ceiling of the meetinghouse. As they writhed on the floor they shouted that the specter was being joined by the specters of John Proctor and two local women, Goodwife Bibber and Goodwife Pope. The Proctors, Bibber, and Pope were sent straight to the Boston jail. Another prisoner was Dorcas Good, Sarah Good's four-year-old daughter, who had apparently confessed to being a witch herself.

First Salem Trial

The first trial in Salem Town marked a significant change in the course of the witchcraft proceedings. The presence of Boston dignitaries, who served as judges and imposed harsh sentences, gave validity to both spectral evidence and the girls' fits as primary proofs of guilt. In addition, Chief Magistrate John Hathorne made a formal statement in court implying that the devil could not take the shape of an innocent person, ruling out any argument that the devil was simply tricking the community by inhabiting otherwise respectable citizens. Consequently, people had the power to accuse anyone they did not like or trust of being a witch simply by claiming that person's specter was tormenting them. Similarly, the girls could cast a shadow of guilt upon accused witches by going into fierce fits when in their presence. Acceptance of these two factors by the courts would have deadly consequences, as it became virtually impossible for the accused to prove their own innocence. Historians do not know for certain if the girls' fits were real, for their dramatic outbursts could have been inspired by actual fear of witches or by the prompting of their own spiteful relatives. After the first trial arrest warrants were issued with increasing rapidity for anyone remotely associated with the charges. Between April 11, 1692 and the beginning of May, warrants were issued for Mary Easty, Edward and Sarah Bishop, Deliverance and William Hobbs, Sarah Wildes, Mary Black, Nehemiah Abbott, Jr., Mary English, and Reverend George Burroughs. This was just the beginning: as innocent people waited in shackles in filthy jail cells, their fates were sealed by the public outrage against witches that boiled above them in the streets and in the courtrooms.

Girls turn on one of their own

On April 11 the group of afflicted girls suddenly turned against Mary Warren, one of their own friends. Warren was the house servant of John and Elizabeth Proctor. On this day, just before Elizabeth Proctor was to appear in court, the girls went into fits in front of a large crowd when Warren approached them. As they fell into their typical fits, Warren also had a particularly violent and bizarre series of seizures. Some of the girls called out that Warren was about to confess to being a witch but that the specters of Corey and Proctor were silencing her. According to *The Salem Witch Trials,* when Warren emerged from her fits she started to say things like "I will speak, Oh, I am sorry for it, I am sorry for it! Oh Lord help me, oh good Lord save me! I will tell! They did, they did! They brought me to it!" She fell into fits again, never clarifying what she had meant and who had brought her to what actions. Was she consumed with guilt over falsifying evidence against her employers and the rest of the victims? Was she implying that the girls had forced her to lie? Historians have found no explanation for this bizarre episode. Warren was taken to a prison cell, where she continued to experience intense fits. The magistrates prodded her for a confession about the Proctors' guilt. Subjected to extreme duress, she finally implicated herself and John Proctor. Warren then lapsed into such a severe state that her legs could not be uncrossed without breaking them.

The Court of Oyer and Terminer

After a month of arrests William Phipps, the new Massachusetts governor, and Boston minister Increase Mather arrived from England with a new provincial charter for the colony (see Chapter 3). On June 2, 1692, Phipps created the Court of Oyer and Terminer (an Old French language term for "To hear and determine"). This court was composed of Lieutenant Governor William Stoughton, Nathaniel Saltonstall, Bartholomew Gedney, Peter Sergeant, Samuel Sewall, Wait Still Winthrop, John Richards, John Hathorne, and, later, Johnathan Corwin. Only Hathorne and Gedney were local people, while the rest of the men came from Boston and Dorchester. All were widely experienced magistrates, and Phipps hoped they would be far enough removed from local tensions to preside over the trials in an objective manner. To the contrary, however, these judges brought their own prejudices and fears about witches, which would surface throughout the hearings.

By this time seventy people were scattered in various jail cells waiting to go to trial. **Bridget Bishop** (see biography entry) was the first to be tried at the new court of Oyer and Terminer. The seventy-year-old wife of local sawmill owner Edward Bishop, she had faced accusations of witchcraft several decades earlier. The trial itself was mainly a rehashing of earlier evidence and accusations, which would be typical in the trials

to follow. Several neighbors claimed that Bishop had murdered local children, while others testified that her specter had been taunting them for quite some time. The most damaging evidence came from two men who had helped her rebuild a portion of her cellar wall, where they claimed to have found witch's puppets made of rags and boar's bristles. As reprinted in *Early American Writing*, by Giles Gunn, Boston minister **Cotton Mather** (see biography and primary source entries) noted in his diary that "There was little occasion to prove the witchcraft, this being evident and notorious [obvious] to all beholders." In other words, Bishop was considered guilty long before she could plead her innocence. She was sentenced to death by hanging, but a legal hitch stood in the way of the Salem courts: at this time Massachusetts no longer had a death penalty for the crime of witchcraft. On June 8 the Massachusetts General Court reinstated the old colonial law that had named witchcraft a capital offense to be punishable by death. Thus the way was cleared for the execution of witches.

Bridget Bishop was the first accused witch to be hanged, on June 10, 1692.
Reproduced by permission of Brown Brothers, Ltd.

On June 10 Bishop became the first accused witch to be hanged in Salem Town. Her execution led to the resignation of magistrate Nathaniel Saltonstall. Frightened by the prospect of attracting negative attention to himself, he quietly left the bench and simply said that the girls' fits and spectral evidence were not good sources for primary evidence. Saltonstall reportedly became a raging drunkard from then on, living the rest of his life in guilt and shame over his involvements in Bishop's sentence. He was replaced by Johnathan Corwin.

As a result of Bishop's hanging and the resignation of a magistrate, Phipps sent a plea for guidance on the issue of spectral evidence to a council of twelve Puritan ministers that included both Increase Mather and his son Cotton. The council urged the courts to act swiftly to remove the threat of witches from the area, but also cautioned them to consider the possibility that Satan may be trying to trick them. Writing for the council, as quoted in *The Salem Witch Trials*, Cotton Mather observed:

> We judge that in the prosecution of these, and all such witchcrafts, there is a need of a very critical and exquisite caution, lest by too much credulity for [belief in] things received upon the Devil's authority there be a door opened for a long train of miserable consequences, and Satan get an advantage over us . . . nevertheless, we cannot but humbly recommend unto the government the speedy and vigorous prosecution [of all witches].

The council of ministers further recommended that the courts disallow the testimony of those who had confessed to witchcraft, limit the use of spectral evidence, and discourage outbreaks of fits among the girls during a trial. This last recommendation resulted in a split between the ministers and the magistrates. The magistrates felt too limited by these new guidelines. The ministers were reluctant to oppose the courts, so their decisions remained weak at best. The ministers could have put a stop to the trials by barring the girls from the courtroom altogether, but their reluctance to anger the judges kept the same basic rules in place. The girls' visible tortures therefore remained the primary source of evidence.

No way out for many victims

On June 13 Sarah Good, Rebecca Nurse, Susannah Martin, Elizabeth Howe, and Sarah Wildes were brought to

trial. Hathorne's sister and brother-in-law testified on behalf of Nurse, and thirty-nine of her former neighbors presented a petition stating that she was a devout Christian. Even Johnathan Putnam, one of her original accusers, signed the petition. (See *The Examination of Rebecca Nurse* in the Primary Sources section.) When the jury declared Nurse "Not Guilty" the courtroom burst into an uproar. The girls and Nurse's other accusers went into hysterics and demanded a retrial. Chief Justice William Stoughton went so far as to ask the jury to reconsider their verdict on the basis of a statement Nurse had made earlier in the trial. At that time a confessed witch, Deliverance Hobbs, had been brought into the courtroom and Nurse had asked, "What, do you bring her? She is one of us." Stoughton convinced the jury to interpret this as a confession. When Nurse was questioned about her statement she paused just slightly too long and her silence was interpreted as guilt. Later she said she was practically deaf and had not heard the question. She explained that she had been surprised to see a fellow

Susannah Martin stood up for herself at her trial, and tried to tell the judges that they were being tricked by the devil.
Reproduced by permission of the Corbis Corporation (Bellevue).

prisoner ("one of us") being brought into the courtroom. This explanation came too late, however, for the jury had already reversed its decision and declared her guilty. Nurse's astonished friends begged the court for a reprieve (pardon). Phipps granted the reprieve, but then the girls went into another series of fits that convinced him to reverse the decision. Following this new verdict, Nurse was unanimously excommunicated (expelled) from the church, an act that symbolized eternal damnation with no chance at justice in God's court. She was also sentenced to hang.

Susannah Martin was the next to take the stand in her own defense. With wit and mockery she rebuked (strongly criticized) the court and jury for admitting spectral evidence as fact (see *The Salem Trials: Interrogation of Susannah Martin* in the Primary Sources section). She also asserted the innocence of the other accused women appearing in court with her. Martin then gave a compelling speech in which she tried to convince the judges that they were being tricked by the devil. The court ignored her entirely and condemned her to hang on the basis of a confession she had made as early as 1669.

Elizabeth Howe's case exposed again the land rivalries behind many of the witchcraft accusations. She had lived most of her life on the contested Topsfield-Ipswich border with her blind husband and two daughters. This unfortunate geographical position had caused major financial disputes, as both towns had attempted to tax the Howe property. The Putnams had been the Howes' primary opponents in many land disputes, although other neighbors had contested their property boundaries. Howe was originally charged with witchcraft on the accusation of a neighbor who claimed his daughter had fallen ill after an argument with Howe. The child complained of being pricked and tormented by Howe. She also had reportedly seeing Howe climbing in and out of an oven as she tortured her. Reverend Samuel Phillips of Topsfield testified that he had overheard a conversation, recounted in *The Salem Witch Trials*, in which Howe asked the child if Howe had ever hurt her. The child had replied, "No, never, and if I did complain of you in my fits I know not that I did so." Phillips then said he had heard the girl's older brother call out from an upstairs window, " Say that Goodwife Howe is a witch! Say she is a witch!" Phillips continued to defend Howe, arguing that the child could easily have been convinced her own neighbor was a witch under pressure from her relatives. Howe's ninety-four-year-old father-in-law then testified on her behalf. He stated that she was the kindest, most helpful member of the family. He went on to describe her devotion to her blind husband, whom she assisted in every aspect of his daily life. Still, neither of these powerful testimonials budged the jury or the court. Howe was found guilty and sentenced to hang. The case of Sarah Wildes was almost identical to that of Howe. Wildes too lived on the treacherous Topsfield-Ipswich border and was considered by her neighbors to be elitist and stingy with her farm equipment. She was swiftly sentenced to hang with Howe.

Hangings on Gallows Hill

The hangings took place on Gallows Hill, outside of Salem Town. On July 19, 1692, Good, Nurse, Martin, Howe, and Wildes were carried by cart out of town on Boston road, past the North River, and to the foot of Gallows Hill. There they experienced abusive treatment from the crowd and the executioner. They were followed by an enormous group of spectators who taunted and threw things at them. Upon reaching the base of the hill they were forced to walk up to the top, to the Hanging Tree. The women had been weakened by starvation and illness during their time in jail, and this last walk was especially difficult for the elderly, such as Nurse. Some were actually too weak to walk and they begged for help from the crowd, but to no avail. Nobody wanted to risk being associated with a witch. As the women made their way up the hill the girls took turns jeering at them and further riling the crowd. One by one the women were told to stand on a wooden crate and insert their heads into the noose of the hanging rope. The executioner, Nicholas Noyes, was famous for his departing taunts to the witches and seemed to enjoy his role in the gruesome spectacle. Hanging was a slow and agonizing way to die: once the crate was kicked out of the way, the victim would drop and thrash in agony for several minutes. If a victim's neck did not break during the fall she would be suffocated and remain conscious for several minutes prior to death. In a few cases the hanging was unsuccessful and Noyes had to start the torturous process over again.

Gallows Hill was the site of most of the witchcraft executions.
Reproduced courtesy of the Library of Congress.

Each of the victims went with as much dignity possible, restating their innocence to the crowd. Noyes tried to elicit last-minute confessions, but none of the women budged from a denial of practicing witchcraft. When Good was waiting to be hanged she gave a powerful speech to Noyes as he taunted her for being a witch, as related in *The Salem Witch Trials,* "I am no more a witch than you are a wizard [magician] and if you take away my life, God will give you blood to drink." (Noyes died years later when he reportedly choked on his own blood.) Following the hangings the bodies were cut from the ropes then dragged to a shallow grave where they were dumped unceremoniously and covered with dirt. Relatives of the victims were charged for all transportation costs to the hill, as well as executioner's fees and burial charges.

The trials continue

During the next wave of trials George Burroughs, John Proctor, George Jacob, Sr., John Willard, and Martha Carrier were all sentenced to hang. Elizabeth Proctor was also found guilty but was allowed to stay in jail until her baby was born. John Proctor was found guilty for little more than defending his wife during her trial. He had burst into the courtroom in a final attempt to testify on her behalf. Abigail Williams had been quick to declare that he was as guilty as his wife, thus providing the magistrates enough evidence to condemn him.

Old and lame George Jacobs was found guilty on the basis of his granddaughter's testimony that he was a wizard. Although she later retracted (took back) her statement, it came too late and the court sentenced Burroughs to hang. According to Frances Hill in *A Delusion of Satan,* he replied to the guilty vedict by saying: "You tax me for a wizard; you may as well tax me for a buzzard. I have done no harm." He defended his innocence all the way to Gallows Hill, where he spoke of Christ's salvation through God. A similar defense came from George Burroughs, who had been accused of being a "Black Minister" by Abigail. As Burroughs stood on the gallows he began with the Lord's Prayer. Since this is the principal Christian prayer, Puritans believed that a witch could not recite it. Many of the onlookers were moved to tears as Burroughs gave a final speech in which he appealed to the spiritual conscience of the people in the crowd. Carrier made similarly emotional appeals. She had been found guilty on the basis of her own two children's evidence against her—evidence that authorities apparently extracted by tying the children's necks to their heels until they made a confession. When Carrier was declared guilty she accused the court and jury of lying and conspiring with the devil. Her children later retracted their so-called confessions when they felt it would be safe to speak, but by this

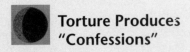

Torture Produces "Confessions"

Martha Carrier was found guilty of practicing witchcraft on the basis of her own two children's evidence against her—evidence that authorities apparently extracted by tying the children's necks to their heels until they made a confession. The Carrier case marked the return of the use of torture to extract confessions. Though not so elaborate as the devices used in Europe (see Chapter 1), torture in the Salem trials often consisted of methods such as those used on the Carrier children. Many people were tied up in contorted and painful positions or forced to stand up for days at a time during an endless series of questions. A more subtle and enduring form of torture was the condition of the jails, into which hundreds of suspects were crammed together without light, food, water, or any form of hygiene. Since many were taken from families that depended upon them for survival, children of the accused often went hungry or died as their parents awaited trial.

time Carrier had already been cut down from the Hanging Tree.

The final phase

On September 9, 1692, six more alleged witches were tried, convicted, and sentenced to hang. They were Martha Corey, Mary Easty, Alice Parker, Ann Pudeator, Dorcas Hoar, and Mary Bradbury. Eight days later Margaret Scott, Wilmot Redd, Samuel Wardwell, and Mary Parker were also sent to Gallows Hill. Several accused witches—Abigail Falkner, Nurse Eames, Mary Lacy, Ann Foster, and Abigail Hobbes—were spared from execution when they finally confessed their guilt. On September 10, Giles Corey was brought to court, but he contested the charges against him and refused to stand trial. The court decided to force him to accept a trial. By law authorities had a right to pile stones on a prisoner's body until he or she acknowledged the court's jurisdiction. Historians suggest that Corey must have known his case was hopeless, and therefore decided to defend the truth by refusing a trial. According to court records, as stones were being piled on top of him he continued to ask for more weight. Corey was slowly crushed to death over the course of nine days; he was finally killed on September 19.

The final hangings took place three days later, bringing the death toll to twenty people. Unfortunately, this did not put an end to the witch-hunts.

As the witch-hunts continued through October more and more people of high social status were being accused and jail cells were filling up throughout the area. Even the wives of Governor Phipps and Increase Mather found themselves accused of being witches. Then public opinion underwent a sudden shift, as people began saying that the accused should be seen as merely being "possessed" rather than bewitched. This was a significant distinction, since a possessed person was not aware of doing the work of the devil. As a result the girls were no longer considered expert witnesses in trials and a sense of caution overtook the courts. This shift was made official when Increase Mather delivered a speech titled "Cases of Conscience Concerning Evil Spirits Personating Men," in which he indirectly cast doubt on the use of spectral evidence and questioned the reliability of the girls' visions. On October 12 Phipps declared a full moratorium on (end to) witch trials. The Court of Oyer and Terminer was dissolved seventeen days later. By then the court had heard thirty-one cases and declared a death sentence for each defendant. Eleven people were still in jails awaiting execution. Eventually five received reprieves after confessing their guilt, while two died in jail before they were set free. One woman was pardoned because of pregnancy, and the rest escaped from jail. Tituba, the first person to be charged and jailed, was never hanged. Samuel Parris apparently sold her into slavery to recover the costs of her jailing and trials.

The last days of the Salem hysteria

Another significant change occurred in October 1692: the English government granted Massachusetts a new charter that gave jury power to all males in the community. Formerly only church members had the right to sit on a jury, thus ensuring that the opinions and beliefs of the church would determine the fate of the accused. Now that juries would be drawn from the general public, who tended to be more aware of social problems than the Puritan elite, the accused stood a better chance of not being put to death. As an extension of this new provision, on November 25 a superior court was created to hear cases. The court did not have its first hearing, however, until a full year later. In the meantime jails were being packed to full capacity as accusations of witchcraft continued to circulate throughout the colony. The general court finally decided to issue an emergency plan to deal with people who were languishing in jail cells. On December 16 the court passed a special act to allow trials for the remaining accused witches.

Several of the judges involved in the new hearings had also sat in the Court of Oyer and Terminer, yet no one ques-

tioned whether these men had sent innocent people to the gallows. Instead the focus was on the use of spectral evidence and the girls' courtroom antics, rather than on the credibility of the judges involved in the previous trials. The girls immediately encountered a different reception when they were called to Gloucester in November for the trial of a young woman who was supposedly possessed by the devil. In their usual fashion the girls declared that the young woman had been bewitched by three other Gloucester women. Yet village officials took no steps to imprison or try the women. On the journey home from Gloucester the girls met with even greater indifference. While crossing a crowded bridge they passed an old woman and proceeded to go into fits. They screamed that the woman was a witch, but to their surprise not a single person reacted to their hysterics—they were treated as if they were invisible. People walked around them and went about their business, causing the girls to realize their reign was ending. When they returned to Salem not one girl had a public fit or made another

The Crucible

In 1953 American playwright Arthur Miller wrote *The Crucible,* a drama based on the Salem witch-hunts. Featuring characters drawn from actual participants in the trials, *The Crucible* addresses the complex moral dilemmas of John Proctor, who is wrongly accused of practicing witchcraft. Through a depiction of the mass frenzy of the witch hunt, Miller examined the social and psychological aspects of group pressure and the effect on individual ethics (knowledge of right and wrong), dignity, and beliefs. The play has been interpreted as a thinly disguised critique of Senator Joseph McCarthy's notorious investigations of communism in the United States in the 1950s. In a personal experience reminiscent of (similar to) the Salem trials, Miller himself was called to testify before the House Committee on Un-American Activities in 1957. Although he admitted that he had attended a meeting of communist writers, he refused to identify anyone he had met there and denied ever having been a member of the Communist Party. As a result, Miller was found guilty of contempt of Congress, a conviction that was later overturned. *The Crucible* is still performed throughout the world and was most recently adapted as a feature film in 1996, with Daniel Day-Lewis starring as John Proctor and Winona Ryder as Abigail Williams.

accusation. With the girls now effectively silenced, the courts acted to free and pardon the remaining prisoners.

On January 3, 1693, during a special trial, charges against thirty of the accused were dismissed on the basis of insufficient evidence, namely the fact that spectral evidence had been the primary evidence against them. When the jury inquired as to how much worth they should grant spectral evidence, Judge William Stoughton responded, as quoted by Frances Hill in *A Delusion of Satan,* "As much as of chips in wort," which meant it should be worth nothing. Twenty-six more people were actually tried, but only three women were found guilty. Since they were developmentally handicapped and mildly retarded, they could not formally defend themselves during the trial. Thus the women became convenient scapegoats: the court was determined to find someone guilty to show that the judges had not been wrong in the previous trials. All three were sentenced to be hanged immediately as a symbolic end to the trials. At this point Phipps stepped in and granted a reprieve for the women as well as five others who were still awaiting executions ordered by the Court of Oyer and Terminer. In response, as recounted by Hill, Stoughton stormed off the bench and screamed in fury: "We were in a position to have cleared the land . . . who is it then that obstructs the course of justice I know not; the Lord be merciful to the country."

The following April the remaining defendants were freed after a superior court hearing in Boston. In May Phipps demanded the discharge of all prisoners awaiting trial, many of whom had been forced to stay in jail until their families could pay their fees. By this time several people had perished in the intolerable conditions and others were so financially ruined that they could not pay for their own freedom. Prisoners were charged dearly for maintenance, clothing, fuel, transport to jail, court and prison fees, discharge from jail, and even reprieve from execution. By autumn people were petitioning for waivers on their fees and were asking to be placed under "house arrest" so they could care for their families or receive the care they needed themselves. Phipps granted an amnesty to some prisoners, but innocent people had already been robbed of property, family, health, money, and social standing. Many did not live to tell the tale or recover from the devastation. Apologies and reprieves from the courts simply came too late. In just one year twenty people had been executed and countless others had lost their lives in jail cells. The Salem tragedy had reached enormous proportions, and nothing could undo the destruction.

For Further Study

Discovery Online—A Village Possessed: A True Story of Witchcraft http://www.discovery.com/stories/history/witches/witches.html. (Accessed July 7, 2000).

Gunn, Giles, editor. *Early American Writing.* New York: Penguin Classics, 1993.

Hill, Frances. *A Delusion of Satan: The Full Story of the Salem Witch Trials.* New York: Doubleday, 1995.

Rice, Earle, Jr. *The Salem Witch Trials.* San Diego, California: Lucent Books, 1997.

Aftermath of the Salem Trials

5

A fter the prisoners awaiting trial on charges of practicing witchcraft were granted amnesty (pardoned) in 1693, the accusers and judges showed hardly any remorse for executing twenty people and causing others to languish in jails. Instead they placed the blame on the "trickery of Satan," thus freeing themselves from any sense of guilt. Jurors and townspeople also managed to maintain a clear conscience by claiming that, after all, many victims had confessed to their "crimes" and that the Salem, Massachusetts, community had been tricked by the devil. Yet families who had lost loved ones and property during the trials were expected to go on with their lives as if nothing had happened. Their attempts to regain social standing and receive financial compensation through formal legal channels took several years.

Judges and accusers show minimal guilt

Eventually a few judges hinted at apologies for their roles in the trials, but they did not assume any real guilt. For instance, Massachusetts governor William Phipps conveniently blamed his lieutenant governor, William Stoughton, who had served as a

Words to Know

bigot: an extrememly prejudiced person

compensation: payment

discontent: unhappiness

hallmark: a distinguishing characteristic

motive: reason

optimism: belief that the future holds good things

outwit: outsmart

rationalism: beliefs based on facts, reason, and logic

reclusive: preferring to be alone

scapegoat: someone or something that is blamed for everything rather than the person or thing that is really at fault

scrutiny: careful inspection

stigma: a mental feeling of shame

judge (see Chapter 4). As early as 1693 Phipps wrote a letter to the British government, quoted by Frances Hill in *A Delusion of Satan*, claiming that Stoughton "Hath from the beginning hurried on these matters with great precipitancy [haste] and by his warrant hath caused the estates, goods, and chattels [movable property] of the executed to be seized and disposed of without my knowledge or consent." Plagued by poor harvests and mild disasters since the onset of the trials, Puritan leaders had begun to worry that God might be punishing them. Consequently some officials made earnest attempts to address the issue. The Massachusetts legislature declared January 14, 1697 a Day of Fasting to commemorate the victims of the trials. On this day, twelve trial jurors signed a petition admitting that they had convicted and condemned people to death on the basis of insufficient evidence. The document stated:

We do therefore hereby signify to all in general (and to the surviving sufferers in especial) . . . that we were sadly deluded and mistaken, for which we are much disquieted and distressed in our minds; and do therefore humbly beg for forgiveness. . . . We do heartily ask forgiveness from you all, whom we have justly offended, and do declare to our present minds, we would none of us do such things again on such grounds for the whole world, praying you to accept this in satisfaction for our offense, and that you would bless the inheritance of the Lord, that he may be entreated for the land. (From Hill, Frances, *A Delusion of Satan*, p. 99.)

The most emotional plea for forgiveness came from **Samuel Sewall** (see biography and primary source entries), one of the magistrates (judges). He went a step further than the jurors by "Taking the blame and shame of it" and asking God to forgive him for his role in the trials. As related in *A Delusion of Satan*, as Sewall stood in front of the congregation of Old South Church in Boston, Massachusetts, his apology was read aloud by Reverend Samuel Willard. Sewall begged God to spare

Samuel Parris Leaves Town

In the wake of the trials Samuel Parris, minister of the Salem Village church, attempted in vain to clear his name and retain his position in the community. As noted in *A Delusion of Satan,* he pointed to the role that deep social conflicts had played in the trials: "I beg, entreat, and beseech you Satan, the Devil . . . may no longer be served by us, by our envy and strifes . . . but that all from this day forward may be covered with the mantle of love and may on all hands forgive each other heartily, sincerely and thoroughly, as we do hope and pray that God, for Christ's sake, would forgive each of ourselves."

In the end, however, Parris deflected the blame onto Satan rather than himself and the Putnam family, all of whom actively promoted the witch hunts and executions. It was too late: his old rivals united with people who had been victimized by the trials and accused Parris of pressuring the judges to accept spectral evidence (claims of seeing a person's spirit committing a foul act which, though unprovable, was used to send a number of people to their deaths). On November 26, 1694, Parris made another speech in the Salem Village church, this time admitting he had been wrong to believe in spectral evidence. Nevertheless, he still tried to hold onto the deeds to the parsonage and parish lands granted him when he came to teh village (see Chapter 3), but his desperation dealt the final blow to his career. In September 1697 a council of ministers forced him to resign and leave Salem.

the rest of the community and to place the punishment on him instead. Yet even Sewall blamed the trickery of Satan, not the true culprits: the deep social conflicts in Salem and the lies told by Elizabeth Parris, Abigail Williams, and the other girls. "Whatever mistakes on either hand have been fallen into, either by the body of this people or any orders of men [they were a] tragedy raised upon us by Satan and his instruments," he maintained. Nonetheless, for the rest of his life Sewall observed a day of fasting each year in atonement for his sins.

Calef blasts bigots

A few participants in the Salem story tried to explain the events in full-length books. For instance, in 1696 John Hale

This wax statue is supposed to represent the torture and ridicule of a witch waiting for execution.
Reproduced by permission of Corbis Corporation (Bellevue).

wrote *A Modest Inquiry,* in which he contended that the witches had been guilty. Although he acknowledged the mixed motives of the community, he justified the executions. In fact, he felt the witch-hunts had ended too early because leaders had been distracted by the escalating social chaos that brought an end to the trials. Boston merchant and trial critic **Robert Calef** (see biography primary sources entries) took the opposite position. In 1697 he wrote *More Wonders of the Invisible World,* in which he attacked the accusers and judges of viciously turning on their own neighbors and friends:

And now to sum up all in a few words, we have seen a bigoted zeal [extreme prejudice] stirring up a blind and most bloody rage, not against enemies or irreligious profligate [irresponsible] persons, but against as virtuous and religious as any . . . and this by the testimony of vile varlets [unprincipled persons] as not only were known before but have been further apparent since by their manifest lives, whoredoms, incest . . . etc. The accusations of these, from their spectral sight being the chief evidence against those that suffered. In which accusations were upheld by both magistrates and ministers, so long as they apprehended themselves in no danger. (From Frances Hill. *A Delusion of Satan,* p. 209.)

Calef's book also attacked religious leaders like **Cotton Mather** (see biography and primary source entries), who encouraged charges of witchcraft rather than trying to determine the truth. Calef aggravated the dispute even further by printing "Another Brand Plucked From the Fire," an account of conversations and written correspondence between Mather and him. Calef attacked Mather for taking supposedly bewitched girls into his own home and encouraging their testimony against accused witches during the trials. Mather was deeply offended by Calef's charges, and he spent the remainder of his life trying to justify his actions. Calef also targeted judges such as Stoughton and chief magistrate John Hathorne for their illegal tactics and prejudicial treatment of accused witches. Neither Stoughton nor Hathorne expressed any sense of remorse or guilt. They never looked back on this period in their careers, and they were never required to account for their roles in the execution of innocent people. Both men remained highly respected and wealthy members of their communities.

Victims ignored by courts

As soon as the trials were over the victims and their relatives pleaded with the courts for financial compensation and social recognition. They had to wait until 1700 for any legal body even to acknowledge their requests, and by this time many families had already been ruined. Accused witch Abigail Falkner was the first person to write a request to the court for a "defacing of the record" emphasizing that she was regarded as a criminal in her community. She noted, according to Frances Hill, that the only testimony in her case had been spectral evidence, which had since lost any legal validity. Despite this fact the courts did not grant Falkner's request, and it continued to delay action on the appeals of other victims as well. In March 1702 frustrated survivors and relatives submitted an extensive petition to the courts asking for formal restitution (restoring) of character. In response the Massachusetts legislature passed a formal bill forbidding the use of spectral evidence, thus implying the innocence of people who had been wrongly convicted and executed—but still not formally clearing their names.

A year and a half later former prisoners and their families tried another tactic. This time they appealed to the Massachusetts General Court, claiming that Elizabeth Parris, Abigail Williams, **Ann Putnam, Jr.** (see biography and primary source entries), and the other girls who started the witchcraft hysteria had been possessed by the devil and therefore their testimony had no legal basis. Again the courts gave no formal response. In May 1709 another petition requested both social and financial remuneration (payment), but once again there was no formal reaction from the courts. In 1710 Isaac Easty presented a memo asking for compensation for the loss of his wife, Mary, one of the twenty people who were executed. As recorded by Francis Hill in *A Delusion of Satan*, Easty acknowledged that nothing could make up for his "sorrow and trouble of heart in being deprived of her in such a manner" and declared that the courts should render justice to him and the families of other victims. Easty's action prompted relatives of executed witches Elizabeth Howe, Sarah Wilde, Mary Bradbury, George Burroughs, Giles and Martha Corey, and Rebecca Nurse to submit similar pleas. At long last the courts granted a sum of 578 pounds (British money) to be split among the petitioners and the families of other victims according to their financial status prior to the tri-

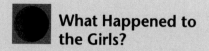

What Happened to the Girls?

Most of the accusers in the Salem trials went on to lead fairly normal lives. Betty Parris, Elizabeth Booth, Sarah Churchill, Mary Walcott, and Mercy Lewis eventually married and had families. Records do not reveal what happened to Abigail Williams, Elizabeth Hubbard, Susannah Sheldon, or Mary Warren. **Ann Putnam, Jr.,** stayed in Salem Village for the rest of her life. Both of her parents died of an unknown infectious disease within months of one another in 1699, leaving Ann in charge of raising her nine younger siblings. In 1706, at age twenty-seven, Ann made a formal apology for her role in the trials when she was admitted as a member of the Salem Village church. (See Putnam's biography entry as well as the full text of her apology in the Primary Sources section.)

als. Again, according to Hill, as a result there was a great disparity in the distribution of the money, with the family of John and Elizabeth Proctor receiving 150 pounds and Elizabeth Howe's relatives being awarded only 12 pounds.

Reverend Green starts healing process

When **Samuel Parris** was forced to resign as the minister of Salem Village church and leave town in 1697 (see biography entry and box on p. 71), he was replaced by Joseph Green. More sophisticated and accepting than his predecessor, Green immediately tried to heal the community. He preached forgiveness in his sermons and even changed the seating arrangement in the church, forcing former enemies to acknowledge one another. He also brought justice to victims who had been ignored by the courts. In 1703 Green formally reversed Martha Corey's excommunication (forced removal) from the church (see Chapter 4), thereby restoring her reputation and assuring the relatives of other executed people that their loved ones would not be damned to hell (according to the Christian concept of eternal punishment for sins after death). In 1712 he revoked the excommunications of Rebecca Nurse and Giles Corey (see Chapter 4). Although Green's efforts helped the community eventually recover from the devastation caused by the trials, Salem remained a symbol of fanaticism and injustice. As time passed the trials became etched into the collective conscience of an emerging nation, a warning against the extremes of human nature.

Englightenment replaces superstition

In the century following the Salem trials, social and political changes taking place in the American colonies had a direct impact on New England. During the early eighteenth century people were struggling to redefine traditional superstitions as the Enlightenment, an intellectual and scientific movement that began in Europe in the seventeenth century, introduced a more rational, reasoned, and ordered concept of the universe. The stronghold of Puritan faith was being replaced by the so-called Age of Reason, which provided no opportunity for hysteria over supernatural powers or the battle between God and the devil. Journals and other accounts show that episodes of suspicion and violence against supposed witches became less frequent throughout the region. Nevertheless, accusations of witchcraft persisted in some places, even into the nineteenth century.

Struggle to abandon old beliefs

Indeed, in 1800 a Protestant minister in Fayette, Maine, wrote in his diary, as recounted in historian John Putnam Demos's book *Entertaining Satan,* that there was "Witchcraft in plenty. A man had been troubled six months and it was thought he must die. He is emaciated [dangerously thin] and often horribly distressed. A Mr. Billings, a Baptist teacher, soon to be ordained, has lost his milk for some time." Numerous similar accounts showed the endurance of ancient superstitions. At the same time, however, people struggled to reconcile their old fears with the new rationalism. In 1799 a farmer from Long Island, New York, also quoted in *Entertaining Satan,* expressed his reluctance to believe in witchcraft:

> It is contrary to my senses and my reason, and ridiculous for me to believe in witchcraft, and was it not for what has happened to me and fallen in the way of observation, I should despise the very idea of spirits having the power to act on or operate on the minds or bodies of creatures.

Yet he went on to blame a local gang of women witches for his misfortune. People still believed that witches could be killed by counter-magic; that is, a victim of witchcraft could easily reverse a witch's curse with his or her own curse, which would harm or kill the witch.

Evil witch replaced by pitiful hag

New Englanders continued to target the same kind of person as a witch: an elderly, reclusive woman remained under

A Case of False Accusation

An episode that occurred in 1720 in Littleton, Massachusetts, was eerily similar to the event that started the Salem witch trials. It began when eleven-year-old Elizabeth Blanchard had visions, went into trances, and acted as if she were "possessed.' She tore at her clothing, disfigured herself, and bit other people. She also reported sensations of being strangled and pricked by invisible hands. Soon Elizabeth's two sisters were exhibiting the same bizarre behavior, and all three girls accused a local woman of putting a spell on them. Littleton townspeople gathered for a meeting and were immediately split on the issue. Their reactions showed the struggle between traditional Puritan and Enlightenment values in New England

According to historian John Putnam Demos, "Some thought [the Blanchard sisters] labored of bodily maladies, others that their minds were disordered . . . others thought them to be underwitted; others that they were perverse and wicked children. But the greater number thought and said that they were under an evil hand, or possessed by Satan. This was the general cry of the town."

Ironically, the accused woman died during the controversy, and the children returned to their normal behavior. Years later, as adults, the three girls confessed to their pastor that they had faked the entire episode to get attention and that they had been "Led by folly and pride into outright deceit."

suspicion, particularly in more rural areas that were isolated from modern trends. Traditional healers were under the strongest scrutiny, just as they had been during the European witch-hunts that started in the fifteenth century (see Chapter 1). A newly emerging medical field, based on the latest scientific theories, however, left no place for women healers in mainstream society. In fact the modern stereotype of the witch began taking shape during the eighteenth century: the image of the powerful, eccentric woman who did the work of Satan— in other words, the witch who had stood trial in Salem only a few decades earlier—was reduced to an ugly, toothless, old hag. As a result the witch became a somewhat laughable figure, merely a useless old woman who was socially isolated and even mentally weak. This is clearly reflected in reports that more harm was done *to* witches than was being done *by* them. The Enlightenment encouraged a sense that ordinary people could outwit these outcasts. The new rational man was therefore more powerful than the old hocus-pocus herbalist. Consequently, witches ceased to provoke real fear and instead provoked ridicule and mockery. Evidence comes from the story of a Reverend Walker in New Hampshire who dismissed notions of witchcraft when townspeople appealed for his help against two local witches. "The most [the townspeople] had to fear from witches was from talking about them; that if they would cease talking about them and let them alone, they would soon disappear," Walker commented, as recorded in John Putnam Demos's *Entertaining Satan*.

A new America

During the eighteenth century social and political changes in the colonies produced a new America. Leaders began promoting youth, vitality, and the self-made man. Having fully embraced the rationalism and optimism of the Enlightenment, they championed the individual who spoke his mind. This was a dramatic shift: whereas outspokenness had cost people their lives in the witch trials, it had now become a respected quality. As communities continued to grow, eccentric townspeople were less important or noticeable, and conflicts between rival families became less prevalent. The notion of individuality replaced fear of outsiders or differences that had often united people against voices of discontent (unhappiness) within the community. Furthermore, social conflict and opinionated debate came to be viewed as healthy rather than threatening. Less often were accusations hurled against those who dared to speak their minds about politics, religion, or even their neighbors. By the mid-1700s the New England of the era of the Salem trials was a fading memory.

Women and child-rearing practices change

Ironically, these changes had an impact on three groups that had been especially vulnerable during the trials, both as accusers and accused: the elderly, women, and children, especially young girls. As youth and progress became the hallmarks of the time, the elderly were regarded as being out

A memorial was erected in Danvers, Massachusetts (what used to be Salem Village) in the names of all that were killed.

Reproduced by permission of the Corbis Corporation (Bellevue).

of touch and unnecessary nuisances. Therefore old people were less likely to be targeted as a threat to the community. Women were now experiencing a new way of life. The woman of the Enlightenment was increasingly confined to the home and for the most part isolated from public life. This loss in status removed the stigma of women being associated with power, mystery, and nature. Now a woman was a passionless, delicate creature, and her body was an embarrassing medical condition over which she had no control. Further, the ancient tradition of the midwife who helped women deliver their babies at home, and who also was the target of witchcraft accusations, was slowly being replaced by the all-male medical establishment.

This unfortunate disempowerment of women did serve to protect them from the superstitions that had made them victims of accusations of witchcraft. This shift was accompanied by changes in child-rearing practices, which in turn influenced the lives of children and teenagers in New

England. The Puritans had raised their children to be silent, obedient, and, most importantly, "broken spirits." During the Enlightenment, however, a child was viewed as morally innocent and thus given freedom to explore and play and be gently nurtured toward adulthood. Adolescence became recognized as a unique stage in life, during which young people were encouraged to be social and to explore their world rather than being closely supervised as potential sinners. Young women were given much greater freedom of motion and encouraged to mingle and socialize prior to marriage. These changes dramatically reduced the boredom, frustration, and anxiety that had characterized the lives of the young girls who were involved in the Salem trials. Consequently, time had eliminated an entire category of people who had played a major role in the tragedy. In short, eighteenth-century Americans no longer needed witches as scapegoats. But they soon encountered other misfortunes and problems, so they found new scapegoats: African Americans, Native Americans, recent immigrants, and anyone else who did not quite fit into the Englightenment ideal.

For Further Study

Demos, John Putnam. *Entertaining Satan*. Oxford: Oxford University Press, 1982.

Gunn, Giles, editor. *Early American Writing*. New York: Penguin Classics, 1993.

Hill, Frances. *A Delusion of Satan: The Full Story of the Salem Witch Trials*. New York: Doubleday, 1995.

Rice, Earle, Jr. *The Salem Witch Trials*. San Diego, California: Lucent Books, 1997.

Starkey, Marion L. *The Devil in Massachusetts: A Modern Enquiry into the Salem Witch Trials*. New York: Doubleday, 1989.

Neo-Paganism

As a result of the Enlightenment, a period of intellectual rationalism (reasoning) that started in seventeenth-century Europe and came to the United States in the eighteenth century, (see Chapter 5), cultural, social, economic, and technological changes continued to push fears of witches into the background. Nevertheless, belief in witchcraft still flourished, particularly among peasant societies in isolated areas of Europe. In the nineteenth century an organized revival of witchcraft, called Wicca, took place in Britain among the Romantics, a social and literary group that rejected the dehumanizing effects of industrialization and tried to recapture a closeness to nature. ("Wicca" is a term for "witch" that has been traced to Germanic words like *wik,* meaning "to bend," or Old English words such as *wiccian,* meaning "to cast spells," and *witan,* or "wise person.") In the early 1900s the British Order of the Druids, who claimed to have roots in pre-Christian Ireland, became one of the first formal movements to declare a revival of witchcraft. According to some scholars, however, the druids of Ireland had actually been teachers and wise men, not witches who engaged in the practice of magic.

British writers Margaret Murray, Robert Graves, and Gerald B. Gardner also helped renew interest in ancient religions and witchcraft. Murray was an Egyptologist (an archaeologist who studies ancient Egypt) who, in the 1920s, wrote extensively about such practices as goddess worship and introduced the concept of the coven, or group of witches (see box on p. 84). Graves was a novelist and poet who based his work on mythology (the study of traditional stories and myths). In 1947 he wrote *The White Goddess,* an anthropological and mythological study of the ancient mother goddess who ruled the moon and controlled fertility (the ability of humans, animals, and plants to produce offspring). Graves claimed that poetry originated from the ritual worship of the White Goddess in ancient societies. Whereas Murray and Graves conducted research and wrote books, Gardner set out to revive the actual practice of witchcraft after becoming inspired by Murray's theories (see box). He claimed to have discovered a surviving witches' coven based on an ancient lineage (line of family descendants) that Murray charted in *The Witch-Cult in Europe* (1921). When anti-witchcraft laws of 1735 were repealed by the British Parliament in 1951, Gardner openly declared himself a witch and started teaching his ideas to an ever-increasing number of students. In 1962 two of his followers, Raymond and Rosemary Buckland, went to the United States to teach "Gardnerian witchcraft." The Gardnerians were instrumental in initiating Neo-Paganism ("neo," meaning new and "paganism," the belief in a higher power other than God), which spread throughout North America, Great Britain, and Scandinavia.

Neo-Paganism recognized as religion

By the 1970s numerous covens and spiritual groups were independently reviving rituals and beliefs based on ancient documents or reinterpretations of myths. Many Neo-Paganists called themselves Wiccans. In 1975 the Covenant of the Goddess (CoG) was formed to incorporate hundreds of separate Wiccan covens and was officially recognized as a church in the United States. The CoG is the largest Wiccan organization, representing a variety of belief systems and practices. Its acceptance by official organizations such as the Internal Revenue Service helped to integrate Wiccans into mainstream American society. At the end of the twentieth century Wicca was the eighth largest religion in the United States, ranking with Christianity, Buddhism, Islam, and other established faiths. This fact is not generally known because many Wiccans observe their rituals in small groups, or even in secret, fearing that they will be attacked as Satan worshipers. Although Wicca and witchcraft are often used interchangeably, the two terms have different meanings. Wicca is a formal Neo-Pagan religion, whereas

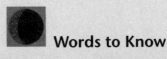

Words to Know

anthropology: study of people and societies

coven: a group of witches

diameter: the measurement around a circle

disciple: follower

landmark: a landmark court decision is a decision that changes the way things are done, or changes the way a law is written

mythology: folklore

Neo-Pagan: a person interested in reviving paganism

offspring: children

priest or priestess: spiritual leader

reinterpretation: another way of seeing or examining something

resurgence: to become popular again

Wicca: witch; also, a formal Neo-Pagan religion

Margaret Murray Influences Neo-Paganism

British Egyptologist Margaret Murray originated the notion that a large pagan underground in Europe and North America had survived extermination during the witch-hunts of the Middle Ages and the seventeenth century. In the 1920s Murray became intrigued by similarities she discovered between ancient documents and writings about paganism in the Middle Ages and the Renaissance (sixteenth century). She based her theory on connections between the pre-Christian horned god of fertility and the Christian concept of the devil. She wrote in the introduction of Gerald B. Gardner's book *Witchcraft Today*:

> I worked only from contemporary records and when I suddenly realized that the so-called Devil was simply a disguised man I was startled, almost alarmed, by the way the recorded facts fell into place, and showed that the witches were members of an old and primitive form of religion, and that the records had been made by members of a new and persecuting form.

In 1921 Murray wrote *The Witch-Cult in Europe*, in which she traced the survival of goddess-worshiping people from ancient times through the witch-hunts of the Middle Ages into the twentieth century. In the book she described the coven, a group of twelve witches headed by the devil, which was supposedly a parody of Jesus of Nazareth, the founder of Christianity, and his twelve disciples (followers). According to Murray, each member of the coven specialized in a distinct form of magic, such as controlling agricultural crops, raising storms, or bewitching humans. The coven concept was adopted by Montague Sommers, a famous Roman Catholic witchcraft scholar in the 1920s and 1930s. *The Witch-Cult in Europe* was generally met with intense criticism and ridicule among Murray's colleagues, however, and her theories remain largely discredited by anthropologists (scientists who study people and societies) and historians. Yet many Neo-Pagan groups call themselves covens, and coven activity became common in the United States and Europe in the 1960s.

witchcraft is the practice of black magic (casting evil spells), which is not used by Wiccans (see Chapter 1). The Neo-Pagan-ists' refusal to form an open, structured religion, however, has created a sense of mystery around Wiccan groups.

Wiccans focus on nature

In an attempt to reunite humans with nature, Neo-Paganists revived the gods and goddesses of ancient religions, such as Mother Earth, Father Sky, the goddess of fertility, and the horned god Pan (see Chapter 1). Wiccans provide the best example of Neo-Pagan practices. Wiccan covens focus on one deity (a god) as a symbolic, unifying force in their rituals; contrary to popular belief, however, Wiccans do not worship the devil, who did not exist before the advent of Christianity (see Chapter 1). The central principle of Wiccan practice is the rede (advice): "An ye harm none, do what ye will"; that is, people are free to act as long as they do not harm others.

Wiccans hold eight primary festivals that are based on the seasons of nature and take place about every forty-five days; these celebrations recall ancient customs dating back thousands of years. The main Wiccan festivals are the winter solstice on December 21, the spring equinox on March 21, and Samhain (Halloween) on October 31—all of them linked to

Early pagans made sacrifices to the female healers and witches.
Reproduced by permission of the Corbis Corporation (Bellevue).

Wicca is a celebration of nature, the seasons, and unity with the universe. *Reproduced by permission of the Corbis Corporation (Bellevue).*

holidays celebrated by other faiths, that have become part of popular culture. Many Wiccans also worship the phases of the moon, ocean tides, and agricultural seasons. Most meet in covens as independent groups headed by a high priestess or priest (spiritual leaders), but all members are given equal status. The traditions and activities of covens vary greatly and allow for flexibility in expression. For instance, some Wiccans adhere to traditional rituals led by a priest or priestess, while others give more freedom to the whole group and rely less upon a leader. Neo-Paganists who do not belong to covens worship independently and may attend special festivals or gatherings several times a year. Many conduct their rituals outdoors, usually in the nude ("sky-clad"), to express their closeness to nature.

A traditional Wiccan ceremony begins with the members of a coven gathering in a circle, usually measuring nine feet in diameter, with candles at four points to show the cardinal directions (north, south, east, and west). An altar consisting of various objects, which represent the energy and power of nature, is located at the center of the circle or at the northern candle point. The ceremony customarily involves lighting the candles and "casting the circle," or creating a "healing" space within the circle of the participants' bodies. Most covens then share a cup of wine, bread, and cookies, and pass special items such as bowls, spoons, incense, and engraved tiles around the circle. The main purpose of the meeting is usually to celebrate a new moon or a holiday, to discuss new ideas, or hold nature-oriented activities. Wiccans observe other rituals, including the act of dedication, in which a person expresses an interest in joining a coven. This is followed by the initiation, in which the person is formally accepted as a Wiccan and takes a Wiccan name. The marriage ceremony is called a "handfasting"; the "parting of ways" ritual marks the end of a marriage. When a baby is born to Wiccan parents, a "Wiccaning" ceremony celebrates the child's entrance into the world; the child is free, however, to choose his or her own faith upon reaching adulthood.

Prejudice and other challenges

The resurgence of Wicca has revived fears and superstitions about witchcraft that have lingered since the witch-hunts of past centuries. Despite greater access to information and education in the modern era, many people believe Wiccans are Satan worshipers, child abusers, and sexual deviants. Frequently encountering harassment and discrimination, Neo-Paganists sought protection through the Civil Rights Act of 1964. The law states: "To be a bona fide [legally authentic or sincere] religious belief entitled to protection under either the First Amendment [constitutional right to freedom of religion] . . . a belief must be sincerely held and within the believer's own scheme of things religious." Although this part of the act is somewhat vague, it inspired several court decisions that gave official recognition to Wiccans. For example, in 1983 the U.S. District Court of Michigan made a landmark decision when it found that three employees of a prison had violated an inmate's constitutional rights by restricting his ability to perform Wiccan rituals. In its ruling the court stated that the prison employees "deprived [the inmate] of his First Amend-

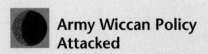

Army Wiccan Policy Attacked

In 1999, three hundred years after the resolution of the Salem witch trials, a controversy arose at Fort Hood, Texas, a U.S. Army base known for tolerance of Wiccan soldiers. The controversy started when the press covered a Wiccan vernal equinox celebration in March 1999 and hate mail began flooding into the camp. Wiccans were called "Satan worshipers," and many soldiers were physically assaulted. The following May, a U.S Congressman from Texas tried to amend a defense authorization bill to prohibit the practice of Wicca at any Defense Department facility, but the bill was promptly dismissed on procedural grounds. In June 1999 thirteen conservative religious groups issued a statement in which they urged their members not to pay taxes or let their children enlist in the military because of the army's tolerance of Wicca. Several other conservative religious groups stepped into the debate and defended both the military and the right of Wiccans to practice their beliefs. The American Freedom Institute made a direct connection between the anti-Wicca campaign and the Salem witch trials, decrying the use of the "freedom for me but not for thee" approach of the coalition.

ment right to freely exercise his religion and his Fourteenth Amendment right to equal protection of the laws," as quoted by the Ontario Consultants on Religious Tolerance.

In 1985 the District Court of Virginia declared that Wicca is a legitimate religion protected by the First Amendment, also cited by the Ontario Consultants on Religious Tolerance:

Members of the [Wiccan] Church sincerely adhere to a fairly complex set of doctrines relating to the spiritual aspect of their lives, and in doing so they have "ultimate concerns" in much the same way as followers of some more accepted religions. Their ceremonies and leadership structure, their rather elaborate set of articulated doctrine [codified beliefs and teachings], their belief in the concept of another world, and their broad concern for improving the quality of life for others gives them at least some facial similarity to other more widely recognized religions.

A similar decision was made by Judge J. Butzner of the Fourth District Federal Appeals Court in 1986 when he agreed that Wiccan beliefs meet the legal definition of a religion and thus require the protection granted to other faiths. The U.S. Army has also recognized Wicca as a legitimate religion. The U.S. Army chaplain's handbook describes the rituals and customs of Wicca in order to guarantee religious freedom.

Neo-Panganism and environmentalism

The twentieth century was a time of great resurgence of pagan-inspired faiths throughout North America. Although many observers have described this movement as a revival of ancient tradition mixed with modern practices, others view Neo-Paganism as an entirely new belief system. Much like traditional healers during the Middle Ages (see Chapter 1), however, Neo-Pagan groups are frequently targeted for being different. Yet according to Margot Adler, author of *Drawing Down the Moon* (1979), a study of Neo-Paganism, they are essentially "Fueled by romantic vision, fantasy, and visionary activities, empowered by a sense of planetary crisis and the idea that such a nature vision may be drowned in an ecocidal nightmare" or ecological destruction. By the 1980s Neo-Paganists were increasingly being identified with other movements such as environmentalism, which attempts to preserve the natural world, and to reestablish the link between humans and nature.

For Further Study

Adler, Margot. *Drawing Down the Moon: Witches, Druids, Goddess-Worshippers, and Other Pagans in America Today.* Boston, Massachusetts: Beacon Press, 1986.

Barstow, Anne Llewellyn. *Witchcraze: A New History of the European Witch Hunts.* San Francisco, California: Harper, 1999.

Buckland, Ray. *Witchcraft From the Inside.* St. Paul, Minnesota: Llewelynn Publications, 1995.

Gardner, Gerald B. *Witchcraft Today.* London: Rider & Co., 1954.

Ontario Consultants on Religious Tolerance. http://www.religioustolerance.org/wic_rel.htm (Accessed July 7, 2000).

Primary Sources

Heinrich Kramer and Jakob Sprenger

From *Malleus Maleficarum (Hammer of Witches)*

Published in 1486
Reprinted in *The Malleus Maleficarum of Heinrich Kramer and James Sprenger* in 1971
Edited by Montague Summers

The *Malleus Maleficarum* (*Hammer of Witches*) was the official handbook for detecting, capturing, torturing, and killing witches (see Chapter 1). It was written in 1486 by Austrian priest Heinrich Kramer (also spelled Kraemer) and German priest Jakob Sprenger, at the request of Pope Innocent VIII, the head of the Roman Catholic Church. The document became the second-best-selling book in Europe for over two centuries (the top best-seller was the Bible). As the main justification for the persecution of witches, the authors relied on a brief passage in the Bible, that states: "Thou shalt not suffer a witch to live" (Exodus 22:18).

The *Malleus Maleficarum* was a three-part work that described witchcraft in elaborate detail. The first part acknowledged the existence of witches and condemned them as demons and heretics (those who break the laws of the church). Much power was given to an accuser, regardless of his or her status in the community, and anyone accused of witchcraft was immediately discredited. The *Malleus Maleficarum* specified that even criminals, the insane, or children could testify against an accused witch once the person was brought to trial.

The second part of the book preyed upon the imaginations and fears of the people by giving evidence of bizarre, disgusting, terrifying, and satanic activities of witches. The *Malleus Maleficarum* placed special emphasis on the relationship between female witches and the devil. Witches were accused of eating children, having sex with the devil, going to sabbaths (mass meetings where witchcraft was performed) with other witches and demons, and having evil connections with ani-

mals known as "familiars." Witches became the human agents of the devil and were held responsible for any number of imagined or real catastrophes.

The conclusion of the *Malleus Maleficarum* outlined the legal procedures required for finding, trying, and executing witches. This section gave free license to lawyers and clergymen, enabling them to take any means necessary to obtain a signed

Based on the guidelines in *Malleus Maleficarum,* accused witches were often checked for things such as moles, warts, and excessive body hair to "prove" that they were witches.
Reproduced by permission of the Peabody Essex Museum.

or verbal confession. To absolve lawyers and clergy themselves from charges of murder, all accused witches were presumed guilty and innocence did not have to be proven. One of the most dangerous aspects of the *Malleus Maleficarum* was that it united the secular (nonreligious) world with the church, creating a murderous and violent regime sanctioned by both law and God. Any accused person could be taken from his or her home to the courts and subjected to various methods of extreme torture. The book prescribed these methods in detail, noting various markings that could "prove" a person was a witch. Such "evidence" included warts, excessive body hair, or extra nipples—all of which gave reason for intense punishment.

The following excerpt, from Chapter II of *Malleus Maleficarum,* describes the three kinds of witches and how they used their powers.

Things to remember while reading *Malleus Maleficarum:*

- The *Malleus Maleficarum* was written almost two hundred years prior to the Salem hysteria.

- The basis for the book was the concept (idea) of *malefecia,* which are mean and evil acts committed by witches or sorcerers. *Malleus Maleficarum* was actually written because Pope Innocent VIII felt that not enough witches were being prosecuted (punished) by the courts for acts of malefecia, and there needed to be a guide that would help people better identify witches and the acts of witchcraft.

From Malleus Maleficarum

*The method by which they profess their **sacrilege** through an open **pact** of **fidelity** to devils varies according to the several practices to which different witches are **addicted**. And to understand this it first must be noted that there are, as was shown in The First Part of the **treatise,** three kinds of witches; namely, those who injure but cannot*

sacrilege: disrespect of something holy

pact: a formal agreement

fidelity: faithfulness

addicted: dependent

treatise: agreement

cure; those who cure but, through some strange pact with the devil, cannot injure; and those who both injure and cure. And among those who injure, one class in particular stands out, which can perform every sort of witchcraft and spell, **comprehending** all that all the others can individually do. **Wherefore,** if we describe the method of **profession** in their case, it will **suffice** also for all the other kinds. And this class is made up of those who, against every instinct of human or animal nature, are in the habit of eating and devouring the children of their own species.

And this is the most powerful class of witches, who **practise innumerable** other harms also. For they raise hailstorms and hurtful **tempests** and lightnings; cause **sterility** in men and animals; offer to devils, or otherwise kill, the children whom they do not devour. But these are only the children who have not been re-born by **baptism** at the **font**, for they cannot devour those who have been baptized, nor any without God's permission. They can also, before the eyes of their parents, and when no one is in sight, throw into the water children walking by the water side; they make horses go mad under their riders; they can transport themselves from place to place through the air, wither in body or in imagination; they can affect Judges and **Magistrates** so that they cannot hurt them; they can cause themselves and others to keep silence under torture; they can bring about a great trembling in the hands and horror in the minds of those who would arrest them; they can show to others **occult** things and future events, by the information of devils, though this may sometimes have a natural cause (see the question: Whether devils can foretell the future, in the Second Book of Sentences); they can see absent things as if they were present; they can turn the minds of men to **inordinate** love or hatred; they can at times strike whom they will with lightening and even kill some men and animals; they can make of no effect the **generative** desires, and even the powers of **copulation,** cause **abortion,** kill infants in the mother's **womb** by a mere exterior touch; they can at times bewitch men and animals with a mere look, without touching them, and cause death; they dedicate their own children to devils; and in short, as has been said, they can cause all the plagues which other witches can only cause in part, that is, when the Justice of God permits such things to be. All these things this most powerful of all classes of witches can do, but they cannot undo them.

comprehending: understanding

wherefore: in which case

profession: occupation

suffice: be enough

practise: practice

innumerable: too many to count

tempests: violent storms

sterility: inability to reproduce sexually

baptism: a religious ceremony where someone is sprinkled with water or dipped in water as they are welcomed into the Christian church

font: a basin that holds holy water for baptisms

magistrates: officials of the court

occult: having to do with magic and supernatural powers

inordinate: more than ordinary

generative: reproductive

copulation: to engage in sexual intercourse

abortion: the birth of a baby before it is old enough to survive

womb: the place in a woman where a baby gows before being born; the uterus

Matthew Hopkins was a well-known witch-hunter.
Reproduced by permission of Corbis/Bettmann.

What happened next . . .

The *Malleus Maleficarum* went on to be used as the definitive handbook for the identification and punishment of witches well into the nineteenth century. It was used as a guiding force for religious writers, and for many of the courts trying to condemn accused witches not only for witchcraft but for heresy. The *Malleus Maleficarum* was also used as a manual for "witch-hunters" such as Matthew Hopkins, who was famous for his witch-hunting tactics, and the number of witches he had captured.

Did you know . . .

• The idea that witches flew on broomsticks was not introduced until the fifteenth century when it was first mentioned in *Malleus Maleficarum*.

• The *Malleus Maleficarum* was the second most popular book sold in Europe and England (second only to the Bible) until the release of *Pilgrim's Progress* by John Bunyan in 1678.

• Heinrich Kramer and James Sprenger were known to have stated that no innocent person could ever be convicted or persecuted for being a witch, as God would not permit it.

For Further Study

Demos, John Putnam. *Entertaining Satan: Witchraft and the Culture of Early New England.* New York: Oxford University Press, 1982.

Kramer, Heinrich, and Jakob Sprenger. *The Malleus Maleficarum of Heinrich Kramer and James Sprenger.* Edited by Montague Summers. New York: Dover Publications, Inc., 1971.

Increase Mather

From *Remarkable Providences* (1684)

**Reprinted in *Major Problems in American
Colonial History* in 1993
Edited by Karen O. Kupperman**

In 1684 the prominent Boston minister Increase Mather (1639–1723) wrote *An Essay for the Recording of Illustrious Providences,* the first work published in the American colonies on the subject of witchcraft. Most commonly referred to as *Remarkable Providences,* it was also the document that helped spark the witch-hunts in New England. Mather was the son of Richard Mather, an English Puritan minister who settled in the Massachusetts Bay Colony in 1635. Increase was born in 1639, his unusual name a product of an era of religious fervor, when Puritans gave their children religiously significant names. "Increase" refers to the belief that God increased his favor for the world by sending his son, Jesus of Nazareth, to save sinners. In 1663, Increase had a son whom he named Cotton after his father-in-law, John Cotton. **Cotton Mather** (see biography and primary source entries) also became a prominent minister in Boston. Increase Mather served as president of Harvard College from 1685 to 1701.

The early government of the Massachusetts Bay Colony, called the General Court, was based on the laws of the Old Testament (the first part of the Bible, the Christian holy

Many accused witches feared that their fate might be burning at the stake, as witches were executed in England. *Reproduced by permission of Archive Photos, Inc.*

Glorious Revolution: a political rebellion in Britian in which King James II, a Catholic, was replaced by Protestant monarchs William III and Mary II.

book). Only men who were church members had the right to vote. The government, simply put, was a small group of men making decisions for everyone else. Within this group, Increase Mather and Cotton Mather enjoyed the highest positions of power. By 1684, however, the English Crown had taken away the New England colonies' right to govern themselves and appointed Sir Edmund Andros (1637–1714), an English governor, to rule over them. The Puritans did not like Andros, and after the **Glorious Revolution** and fall of King James II (1633–1701) in 1688–89, Andros was removed from office. The New England colonies fell into a period of unrest, and Increase Mather went to England in an effort to obtain a new charter (contract granting the right to form a government).

The following excerpt from *Remarkable Providences* describes events in the case of Ann Cole from Hartford, Connecticut. Described as a pious woman overtaken by the spirit of the devil, Cole was the victim of visions, hysterics, and bodily possession. She identified a husband and wife, along with

The practice of dunking or "ducking" an accused witch was a quite popular test, although not always as safely done as pictured here.
Reproduced by permission of the Corbis Corporation (Bellevue).

several others, as being the witches responsible for her bewitchment. The husband and wife were executed, while the others fled for their lives. An interesting element of this account is that two people were subjected to the water test. It was a popular belief at the time that witches would float in water, rather than sink like "non-witches." To determine whether the two suspects were witches, they were bound and thrown into the water, only to half sink and half swim. It is noted that a bystander, who suggested that anyone bound in such a way would float, was himself tied up and put into the water. He sunk straight to the bottom. While floating was not used as evidence against the two accused witches, they decided to flee for their lives. They were never seen again.

Things to remember while reading
Remarkable Providences:

- Mather's purpose in writing *Remarkable Providences* was that he feared the Puritans were becoming too interested in science, commercialism, and individualism, and were therefore forgetting the importance of their religious beliefs.

- Those who had held onto Puritan ideals felt that King Philip's War (1675–76), a bloody conflict with the Native Americans, and recent smallpox epidemics were judgments from God upon the moral decline in New England. *Remarkable Providences* was meant to serve as a graphic reminder of the evil forces at work in the colonies. After hearing about numerous incidents of witchcraft, Mather was inspired to compile this record of eyewitness accounts.

- Like all Puritans, Mather believed that the colonies were a battleground of good and evil, and that evil was winning. He also believed *Remarkable Providences* would provide the proof.

From Remarkable Providences

*Inasmuch as things are **preternatural,** and not accomplished without **diabolical** operation, do more rarely happen, it is a pity but that they should be observed. Several accidents of that kind have happened in New England, which shall here faithfully relate, so far as I have been able to come unto the knowledge of them.*

*Very remarkable was that **Providence** wherein Ann Cole of Hartford in New England was concerned. She was, and is accounted, a person of real **piety** and **integrity;** nevertheless, in the year 1662, then living in her fathers house (who has likewise been **esteemed** a godly man), she was taken with very strange fits, wherein her tongue was improved by a **daemon** to express things which she herself knew nothing of . . . she likewise declared, that the devil first appeared to her in the form of a deer or **fawn,** skipping about her, wherewith she was not much **affrighted,** and that by degrees he became very familiar, and at last would talk with her; moreover, she said that the devil had frequently the **carnal knowledge** of her body; and that the witches had meetings at a place not far from her house; and that some appeared in one shape, and others in another; and one came flying amongst them in the shape of a crow. Upon this confession, with the other **concurrent** evidence, the woman was executed; so likewise was her husband, though he did not **acknowledge** himself guilty.*

preternatural: beyond what is normal

diabolical: devilish or satanic

providence: the control and protection of God

piety: religious devotion

integrity: honesty

esteemed: respected as

daemon: demon

fawn: a baby deer

affrighted: frightened

carnal knowledge: to know someone sexually

concurrent: at the same time

*Other persons accused in the discourse made their escape. Thus doth the devil use to serve his clients. After the suspected witches were either **executed** or fled, Ann Cole was restored to health, and has continued well for many years, approving herself a serious Christian. There were some that had a mind to try whether the stories of witches not being able to sink under water were true; and accordingly a man and woman, mentioned in Ann Cole's Dutch-toned **discourse**, had their hands and feet tyed, and so were cast into the water, and they both apparently swam after the manner of a **buoy**, part under, part above the water. A by-stander, imagining that any person bound in that **posture** would so born up, offered himself for trial; but being in the like manner gently laid on the water, he immediately sunk right down. This was no legal **evidence** against the suspected persons, nor were they **proceeded against** on any such account; however, doubting that an halter would **choak** them, though the waters would not, they very fairly took their flight, not having been seen in that part of the world since. Whether this **experiment** were lawful, or rather superstitious and magical, we shall **enquire** afterwards.*

acknowledge: recognize

executed: killed as a punishment for a crime

discourse: conversation

buoy: float

posture: position

evidence: proof

proceeded against: prosecuted in court

choak: choke

experiment: scientific test

enquire: also inquire; find out

What happened next . . .

While Mather had supported the witch-hunts and resulting trials, by 1693 he had had a drastic change of heart. Mather was not alone in reversing his position. Many other leaders, such as minister Samuel Willard—an early advocate of the trials who, ironically, was accused of witchcraft himself—realized the accusations were ridiculous. Using his political influence and position as head of the Ministerial Association, Mather waited to speak out until the Salem trials had been suspended at the end of the summer. He called the judges and governor together, knowing that they would listen to him. He had not officially expressed his views since writing *Remarkable Providences,* in which he had supported the judges' decisions. Seeing that random accusations were sending people to jail—and many to their deaths—with little or no "evidence" against them, Mather called for a halt to the executions. He presented his new work, entitled *Cases of Conscience,* on October 3, 1693. In it he called into question the decisions and the lack of Christian charity (goodwill)

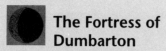

The Fortress of Dumbarton

There is a legend recorded as early as the year 388 B.C. that tells the story of a group of witches that were pursuing Saint Patrick near Glasgow, Scotland, to punish him for offending the devil with his holiness. The tale has Patrick jumping into a small boat on the Clyde River and escaping to Ireland, while the witches stood angrily on the banks, unable to cross into the water. Supposedly, they were so mad that they pulled the top off one of the nearby hills and tried to hurl it at the saint as he made his escape. However, their strength and aim were so poor that the hilltop fell right to the ground, forming a boulder that was later turned into a fortress (the Fortress of Dumbarton).

exercised by the juries in the Salem trials, noting that without overwhelming proof the courts should not have handed down death sentences. Mather called the trials a mistake and urged others to see the error of their ways. *Cases of Conscience* was instrumental in bringing the executions to an end. Within five months, all accused "witches" were set free and the executions were stopped.

Did you know . . .

• While the water test for witchcraft was supposed to determine whether one was guilty of being a witch, the accused often found the test deadly regardless of the findings. Many of the tests involved the accused being bound (legs and hands tied), and sometimes being placed in a bag that had been tied at the end, before being tossed into the water. Unfortunately, if the accused was fortunate enough to float, they were "guilty" of being a witch. If they sank, they were found innocent, but often drowned before anyone could get them out of the water.

• Legend says that witches are also unable to cross running water, such as in a stream, river, or brook (see box)

For Further Study

Demos, John Putnam. *Entertaining Satan: Witchcraft and the Culture of Early New England*. New York: Oxford University Press, 1982.

Discovery Online—A Village Possessed: A True Story of Witchcraft. http://www.discovery.com/stories/history/witches/witches.html (Accessed July 7, 2000).

Hansen, Chadwick. *Witchcraft at Salem*. New York: George Braziller, 1969.

Kupperman, Karen O., ed. *Major Problems in American Colonial History*. New York: Heath, 1993.

Sharpe, C. K. *A History of Witchcraft in Scotland*. Glasgow: Thomas D. Morison, 1884.

Cotton Mather and Ezekiel Cheever

The Salem Trials: Interrogation of Susannah Martin

Reprinted in *Eyewitness to America* in 1997
Edited by David Colbert

C otton Mather, a Boston minister and a strong supporter of witch-hunts, and Ezekial Cheever, a court clerk, wrote an account of the Salem trials of 1692-93. The following excerpt shows a typical exchange, in this case between a magistrate (judge; here unnamed) and an accused witch, Susannah Martin. Mather and Cheever supposedly provided a "report" on the Salem trials, yet Mather in particular was later faulted for fueling the witch-hunt mania. The account of the interrogation of Martin is an example of how Mather and Cheever presented events from a biased point of view.

Things to remember while reading
Interrogation of Susannah Martin:

- Susannah Martin was a sixty-seven-year-old widow who freely spoke her mind and denied all charges against her.

- Note that, in the opening of this excerpt, Mather and Cheever had already concluded Martin was a witch. They saw spectral (ghostly) evidence in her behavior: "The cast of Martin's eye struck people to the ground, whether they saw that cast or not." In other words, she had put a spell

Although the afflicted girls we supposedly struck to the ground when Susannah Martin looked at them, she strongly denied all charges against her.
Reproduced by permission of Archive Photos, Inc.

on the witnesses by giving them the "evil eye." (Believers in the supernatural thought a witch was capable of inflicting harm with a single glance.)

- During the interview with the magistrate Martin engaged in extensive word play, evading his questions and leaving his statements open to interpretation. Their exchange is an example of the Puritan belief that witches could make evil spirits invade the body of a human being. For instance, the magistrate referred to "their Master" (the devil), "Black Art" (witchcraft), and Martin's "Appearance" (the form she took as a witch).

From Interrogation of Susannah Martin

*Susannah Martin pleaded Not Guilty to the **indictment** of witchcraft brought in against her.*

indictment: formal accusation

*The evidence of many persons very sensibly and **grievously bewitched** was produced. . . .*

The cast of Martin's eye struck people to the ground, whether they saw that cast or not.

*These were among the passages between the **Magistrates** and the Accused:*

MAGISTRATE: *"Pray, what **ails** these people?"*

MARTIN: *"I don't know."*

MAGISTRATE: *"But what do you think ails them?"*

MARTIN: *"I don't desire to spend my judgement upon it."*

MAGISTRATE: *"Don't you think they are bewitched?"*

MARTIN: *"No, I do not think they are."*

MAGISTRATE: *"Tell us your thoughts about them then."*

MARTIN: *"No, my thoughts are my own, when they are in;*
but when they are out they are another's. Their Master—"

MAGISTRATE: *"Their Master? Who do you think is their Master?"*

MARTIN: *"If they be dealing in the **Black Art**, then you may*
know as well as I."

MAGISTRATE: *"Well, what have you done towards this?"*

MARTIN: *"Nothing at all."*

MAGISTRATE: *"Why, 'tis you or your **Appearance**."*

MARTIN: *"I cannot help it."*

MAGISTRATE: *"Is it not your Master? How comes your*
Appearance to hurt these?

MARTIN: *"How do I know? He that appeared in the shape of*
Samuel, a glorified Saint, may appear in anyone's shape."

*It was noted that in her, as in others like her, that if the **afflicted** went to approach her, they were flung down to the ground. And, when she was asked the reason of it, she said, "I cannot tell. It may be the Devil bears me more **malice** than another."*

grievously: causing grief

bewitched: to have a spell cast over

Magistrates: officials of the court

ails: to be ill

Black Art: evil magic, witchcraft

Appearance: the form taken when a witch

afflicted: one in great distress

malice: harm

What happened next . . .

Along with many other accused witches, after this interrogation Martin was found guilty and later hanged. She was one of twenty victims of the Salem hysteria.

Did you know . . .

- There is a memorial in Amesbury, Massachusetts, in memory of Susannah Martin. The plaque on a stone commemorating her memory stands on the former site of Martin's home, and states: "Here stood the house of Susanna Martin. An honest, hardworking, Christian woman. Accused as a witch, tried and executed at Salem, July 19, 1692. A martyr of superstition."

For Further Study

Colbert, David, ed. *Eyewitness to AMerica*. *New York: Pantheon Books, 1997.*

Discovery Online—A Village Possessed: A True Story of Witchcraft. http://www.discovery.com/stories/history/witches/witches.html (Accessed July 7, 2000).

Hansen, Chadwick. *Witchcraft at Salem*. New York: George Braziller, 1969.

Hill, Frances. *A Delusion of Satan: The Full Story of the Salem Witch Trials.* New York: Doubleday, 1995.

Kallen, Stuart A. *The Salem Witch Trials*. San Diego, California: Lucent Books, 1999.

Rebecca Nurse

The Examination of Rebecca Nurse (1692)

**Reprinted in *Major Problems in American Colonial History* in 1993
Edited by Karen O. Kupperman**

Rebecca Nurse was an ailing seventy-one-year-old great-grandmother and faithful Salem village church member when she was arrested as a witch in March 1692 (see Chapter 4). Although little is known about her early life, records show that she was born Rebecca Towne in Yarmouth, England, and baptized on February 21, 1621. During her childhood her family moved to Massachusetts and settled in the village of Topsfield. She married Francis Nurse, a farmer, and they rented a large house on 300 acres of land near Salem Village; they had fours sons and four daughters. (The restored Nurse homestead still stands; it has been designated as an historical site.) In 1678 the Nurses obtained the title to the house and land, and over the next fourteen years they became highly respected members of the community. Then in February 1692 Abigail Williams, Elizabeth Parris, **Ann Putnam, Jr.**(see biography and primary source entries), and other young girls claimed they were being attacked by the specters (spirits) of several women, whom they accused of practicing witchcraft. In March 1692 Putnam interrupted a church service and tar-

Many older women were being accused of witchcraft because they lived alone and often kept to themselves.

Reproduced by permission of the Corbis Corporation (Bellevue).

geted Rebecca Nurse as one of the principal witches (see Chapter 3). Ann Putnam, Sr. also began accusing Nurse of witchcraft (see primary source entry). The Nurses immediately stopped attending church. On March 23, 1692, Rebecca Nurse was arrested and sent to the Salem jail even though she had been ill and was confined to her bed.

Things to remember while reading *the Examination of Rebecca Nurse:*

- Historians have concluded that long-standing boundary disputes between the Putnam family and other Salem villagers (see Chapter 4) played a major role in Nurse's arrest. Although her husband had not been an active member of the anti-Putnam group, he had had conflicts over land with Nathaniel Putnam, a relative of Thomas Putnam, who was the father of Ann Putnam, Jr., and himself a main force in the witch-hunts.

- Abigail Williams was a niece of **Samuel Parris** (see biography entry), an ally of the Putnams, she and lived in the Parris household, which was the center of witchcraft allegations.

- Nurse's own family, the Townes, had been bitter enemies of the Putnams; her sisters, Sarah Cloyce and Elizabeth Procter, were soon arrested as witches.

From The Examination of Rebecca Nurse

In the following excerpt from the preliminary hearing held on March 24, 1692, the day after her arrest, Nurse is questioned by chief magistrate John Hathorne (spelled "Harthorn" here). People giving evidence against her are Abigail Williams, Ann Putnam, Jr., Ann Putnam, Sr., Edward Putnam (brother of Thomas Putnam), Thomas Putnam, and Salem villagers Henry Kenney, Mary Walcott, and Elizabeth Hubbard. The questions and answers were recorded by a court clerk (reporter), who inserted commentary about the proceedings.

*Mr. Harthorn: "What do you say (speaking to one **afflicted**), have you seen this woman hurt?"*

[Ann Putnam] "Yes, she beat me this morning."

[Harthorn] "Abigail [Williams], have you been hurt by this woman?"

afflicted: to be suffering

[Abigail] "Yes."

Ann Putnam, in a **grevious** fit, cried out that she hurt her.

[Harthorn] "Goody Nurse, here are two—Ann Putnam the child and Abigail Williams—complains of your hurting them. What do you say to it?"

[Nurse] "I can say before my Eternal Father, I am innocent, and God will clear my innocency."

[Harthorn] "Here is never a one in the **assembly** but desires it. But if guilty you be pray God **discover** you."

[Court clerk] Then Hen[ry] Kenney rose to speak.

[Harthorn] "Goodman Kenney, what do you say?"

[Court clerk] Then he entered his **complaint** and farther said that since this Nurse came into the house he was twice seized with an amazed condition.

[Harthorn] "Here are not only these, but here is [Ann Putnam, Sr.] the wife of Mr. Tho[mas] Putnam who **accuseth** you by **creditable** information, and that both of tempting her to **iniquity** and of greatly hurting her."

[Nurse] "I am innocent and clear, and have not been able to get out of doors these 8 or 9 days."

[Harthorn] "Mr. Putnam, give in what you have to say."

[Court clerk] Then Mr. Edward Putnam gave in his **relate**.

[Harthorn] "Is this true, Goody Nurse?"

[Nurse] "I never afflicted a child, never in my life."

[Harthorn] "You see these accuse you. Is it true?"

[Nurse] "No."

[Harthorn] "Are you an innocent person, relating to this witchcraft?"

[Court clerk] Here Tho[mas] Putnam's wife cried out: Did you not bring the Black man with you? Did you not bid me tempt God and die? How **oft** have you eat and drunk your own **damnation**? What do you say to them?"

[Nurse] "Oh Lord, help me,["] and spread out her hands, and the afflicted were grievously **vexed**.

greivous: causing severe pain or grief

assembly: group of people gathering together for worship or legislation

discover: save

complaint: charges

accuseth: accuse; to blame

creditable: worthy of belief

iniquity: wickedness

relate: story

oft: often

damnation: state of being condemned

vexed: distressed

[Harthorn] "Do you see what a **solemn** condition these are in? When your hands are loose, the persons are afflicted."

[Court clerk] Then Mary Walcott (who often **heretofore** said she had seen her, but never could say, or did say, that she either pinched or bit her, or hurt her) and also Elis[abeth] Hubbard, under the like circumstances, both openly accused her of hurting them.

[Harthorn] "Here are these 2 grown persons now accuse you. What say you? Do not you see these two afflicted persons, and hear them accuse you?"

[Nurse] "The Lord knows. I have not hurt them. I am an innocent person."

solemn: serious

heretofore: until the present time

What happened next . . .

During the hearing many of Nurse's neighbors spoke in her behalf, vehemently proclaiming that she was a good citizen and the least likely person to engage in witchcraft. Nevertheless, she was brought to trial on the basis of spectral evidence—the girls' claim that she had afflicted them through her spirit—and the testimony of mulitple witnesses. Initially Nurse was found "not guilty," but Massachusetts Governor William Phipps bowed to pressure and ordered a second trial (see Chapter 4). Historians speculate that Nurse's deafness, a condition she developed in later years, prevented her from adequately responding to questions. As a result, in spite of her continued protestations of innocence, the jury finally concluded that she was lying and found her guilty. After being excommunicated from the church, Nurse was hanged on July 19, 1692, along with four other convicted witches.

Did you know . . .

- Many of the bodies of the accused and executed witches were buried in shallow, unmarked graves. However, there is historical evidence that the body of Rebecca Nurse was

Most of the accused witches lost their property while in jail, and their families were unable to reclaim it, even after their deaths. This is the house of Rebecca Nurse. *Reproduced by permission of the Corbis Corporation (Bellevue).*

secretly removed from its grave and given a proper burial. This grave still lacked any marking, for fear that someone might desecrate (violate or vandalize) the site.

For Further Study

Kupperman, Karen O. *Major Problems in American Colonial History.* New York: Heath, 1993.

Ogram's 17th Century New England with special emphasis on The Salem Witchcraft Trials of 1692. [Online] http://www.ogram.org/17thc/index.shtml (Accessed July 7, 2000).

Rice, Earle, Jr. *The Salem Witch Trials.* San Diego, California: Lucent Books, 1997.

Starkey, Marion L. *The Devil in Massachusetts: A Modern Enquiry into the Salem Witch Trials.* New York: Doubleday, 1989.

Ann Putnam, Sr.

The Testimony of Ann Putnam, Sr. against Martha Corey and Rebecca Nurse (1692)

Reprinted in *Major Problems in American Colonial History* in 1993
Edited by Karen O. Kupperman

As the New England winter tightened its icy grip, February 1692 drew to a close in Salem, Massachusetts. Two more girls—Elizabeth Hubbard and **Ann Putnam, Jr.**—joined Elizabeth (Betty) Parris and Abigail Williams in having fits and seeing visions. At the time of her "bewitchment," Ann Putnam, Jr. was only twelve years old (see her biography and primary source entries). She was the daughter of Ann Putnam, Sr. and Thomas Putnam, a local farmer who had become quite prosperous. The Putnam family was one of the largest and most powerful in Salem Village, and Thomas's wealth made him an ally of the Reverend Samuel Parris. Suspicions that witchcraft had afflicted his daughter, and later his wife, made Thomas Putnam a strong force in the arrests of accused witches.

Unlike some of the other village girls who took part in the story-telling sessions at the Parris household that ultimately led to accusations of witchcraft, Ann Putnam, Jr. lived with both of her parents. While two-parent households are usually beneficial to children, there is evidence that the unstable behavior of Ann Putnam, Sr. had a devastating effect on the Putnam family—and, ultimately, the entire Salem community. The elder Ann was a disinherited daughter; her father had been

Much of the witchcraft trials, testimonies and depositions took place in the Salem Village meetinghouse. This is a sketch of the original meetinghouse.

Reproduced by permission of the Corbis corporation (Bellevue).

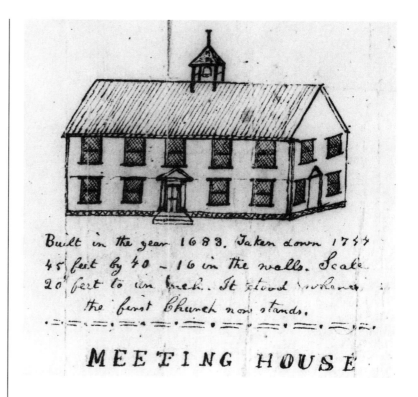

Built in the year 1683. Taken down 1755. 45 feet by 40 - 16 in the walls. Scale 20 feet to an inch. It stood where the first Church now stands.

MEETING HOUSE

wealthy, but when he died she got nothing. The money from his estate was divided between his wife and sons. Ann tried unsuccessfully to sue for her inheritance, and as the years passed she grew more embittered. She married Thomas Putnam after moving to Salem with her sister. When her sister's three children died in quick succession, followed shortly by the sister herself in 1688, Ann's mental stability was severely shaken and she went into a decline. By March 1692 she was suffering from violent fits and claiming to be haunted by specters.

Following is an excerpt from the deposition given by Ann Putnam, Sr. on May 31, 1692, in which she described the "tortures" inflicted upon her by "witches" Martha Corey (also spelled Cory) and Rebecca Nurse. They had also been accused by Ann Putnam, Jr. Both women were upstanding members of the community, yet they were also outspoken in their opposition to the witch-hunts. Corey, who was sixty-five years old, was the fourth person and the first church member to be named as a witch. Nurse was seventy-one, deaf, and bedridden. They were arrested and eventually executed on the basis of the Putnams' charges against them.

Things to remember while reading
The Testimony of Ann Putnam, Sr.:

- This deposition was taken at a time when language differed slightly from what it is today. In some places you will see "th" denoting past tense where in today's language you might see a "d" or an "ed." An example of this would be "testifieth" rather than "testified."

- The Putnams had long been bitter enemies of the Towne family, and therefore enemies of Rebecca Nurse, who's maiden name was Towne. Many historians have speculated that many of the accused witches were put to death for these long-standing disputes that they had with some part of the Putnam family or Putnam family friends.

From The Testimony of Ann Putnam, Sr.

*The **deposition** of Ann Putnam, the wife of Thomas Putnam, aged about 30 years, who testifieth and saith that on the 18th March 1692, I being **wearied** out in helping to tend my poor **afflicted** child [Ann Jr.] and maid, about the middle of the afternoon I lay me down to bed to take a little rest; and immediately I was almost pressed and choked to death, that, had it not been for the mercy of a gracious God and the help of those that were with me, I could not have lived many moments; and presently I saw the **apparition** of Martha Corey, who did torture me so as I cannot express, ready to tear me all to pieces, and then departed from me a little while; but before I could recover strength or well take breath, the apparition of Martha Corey fell upon me again with dreadful torture, and hellish temptations to go along with her. And she also brought to me a little red book in her hand and a black pen, urging me **vehemently** to write in her book; and several times a day she did **greviously** torture me, almost ready to kill me.*

*And on the 19th March, Martha Corey again appeared to me; also Rebecca Nurse, the wife of Francis Nurse, Sr.; and they both did torture me a great many times this day with such great tortures as no tongue can express, because I would not yield to their hellish temptations, that, had I not been upheld by an Almighty arm, I could not have lived [the] night. The 20th March being **sabbath-day**, I had a great deal of **respite** between my fits. 21st March being the day of the*

deposition: a testimony that is taken under oath that is written down as an official record

wearied: tired

afflicted: suffering

apparition: spirit

vehemently: forcefully

greviously: causing severe pain or grief

sabbath-day: holy day

respite: rest

examination: questioning

magistrates: officers of the court

meetinghouse: a large building for general gatherings and meetings

examination of Martha Corey I had not many fits, though I was very weak, my strength being as I thought, almost gone. . . . I was several times in the morning [24 March] afflicted by the apparition of Rebecca Nurse, but most dreadfully tortured by her in the time of her examination, insomuch that the honored magistrates gave my husband leave to carry me to the meetinghouse; and as soon as I was carried out of the meetinghouse doors, it pleased Almighty God, for his free grace and mercy's sake, to deliver me out of the paws of those roaring lions, the jaws of those tearing bears [so] that ever since that time they have not had the power so to afflict me, until this 31st May 1692.

What happened next . . .

Due in part to Ann Putnam, Sr.'s testimony, both Martha Corey and Rebecca Nurse were hanged for supposedly practicing witchcraft. In 1699, both Ann, Sr. and her husband died of an unknown infectious disease within months of one another. At the time, many speculated that they had been cursed by God for their false accusations during the trials.

Did you know . . .

- Black cats were supposedly the favored form of familiars (demons in animal form) in the middle ages. This led to the popular belief (still held today) that black cats bring you bad luck, and led to mass cat massacres in medieval Europe.

- It was said that during the witchcraft trials and interrogations, if a fly flew into the room then the accused was assumed to be a witch, and the fly her familiar.

For Further Study

Kupperman, Karen O. *Major Problems in American Colonial History.* New York: Heath, 1993.

Rice, Earle, Jr. *The Salem Witch Trials.* San Diego, California: Lucent Books, 1997.

The Salem Witch Museum. [Online] http://www.salemwitchmuseum.com/ (Accessed July 7, 2000).

Starkey, Marion L. *The Devil in Massachusetts: A Modern Enquiry into the Salem Witch Trials.* New York: Doubleday, 1989.

Thomas Knowlton

Witchcraft 1687: The Deposition of Thomas Knowlton against Rachel Clinton

Reprinted in *Entertaining Satan: Witchcraft and the Culture of Early New England* in 1982 By John Putnam Demos

Long before the Salem witchcraft trials in 1692–93, Puritans had been blaming witches for problems—economic hardship, epidemic illnesses, political conflict, and social unrest. In fact, during the second half of the seventeenth century charges of witchcraft became rampant in New England communities. Usually, but not always, women were the targets of the charges, and frequently these women lived alone either because they were unmarried, had been widowed, or had been deserted by their husbands. Some had been prosperous citizens who fell on hard times and thus became outsiders. One such woman was Rachel Clinton (see biography entry) of Ipswich, Massachusetts, who was accused of witchcraft in the mid-1680s, around the time prominent Boston Minister Increase Mather's *Remarkable Providences* (see primary source entry) added fuel to the witch-hunt frenzy.

Clinton moved to Ipswich from England with her parents, Richard and Martha Haffield, in 1635. Richard had five daughters, two from a previous marriage and three with Martha. (Rachel therefore had two half-sisters and two sisters of full relation.) The Haffields lived as prosperous members of the community until Richard died in 1639. He left a will that was intended to prevent any conflicts over the estate, giving all the children equal amounts of his property. Nevertheless, there was a continued battle over the settlement and by 1665, when all of Rachel's sisters were married, Rachel and her mother were living together in a small cottage. As a result of unusual behavior, Martha Haffield was certified as insane and unable to care for herself financially. The local court put Thomas White, the husband of Rachel's sister Ruth, in charge of the estate.

Around 1666 Rachel married Lawrence Clinton, an indentured servant who had several years left on his contract. An indentured servant was an immigrant who had signed a contract to work for an employer for a specified number of years in exchange for free passage to America. The servant did not have to serve the remainder of his or her time if someone compensated the employer for his loss of the servant. Rachel therefore used money from her inheritance to pay Lawrence's employer. White felt Rachel did not have the right to the family's money, however, so he decided to take her to court. After years of legal battles, Rachel lost not only her house and money but also good relations with her family. She also lost her husband, whom she divorced after a series of domestic problems, and by 1681 she was alone. The once wealthy and respectable Clinton was now relying on public support. For years she felt betrayed by the town and her family, who had watched her lose everything. Then, in 1687, she was charged with being a witch.

Sometime in 1687 Ipswich residents were invited to give sworn court testimony against Clinton. According to their complaints, people fell dead when she walked past them, and she frequently turned into a dog, cat, or turtle in order to cast spells on upstanding members of the community. (A popular superstition was that a witch could inhabit the body of an animal and work evil spells in the form of that animal; this was called becoming a "familiar.") The following deposition, given by a man named Thomas Knowlton, describes Clinton going to a household and asking for food and drink. When her request was refused, she reacted violently. In response, several townspeople claimed they suffered pains and ailments caused by her witchcraft. Clinton was then arrested, tried, convicted, and imprisoned as a witch.

Things to remember while reading *The Deposition of Thomas Knowlton:*

- At this time in history it was very difficult for women to own property. It had to be left to them by their husbands when they died, and even then the government often found ways of taking the property away and giving it to some male relative.

Rachel Clinton was said to have been seen flying around the village at night with her familiar.
Reproduced by permission of the Gamma Liaison Network.

- For women of this time, it was often the case that one would be declared incompetent (unable to manage your own life or take care of yourself) or insane for something as simple as speaking boldly in public or disagreeing publicly with your husband.

From The deposition of Thomas Knowlton

*The **deposition** of Thomas Knowlton, aged 40 years, sayeth that about three weeks ago [when] Mr. John Rogers and his wife were gone to Boston . . . Rachel, the wife of Lawrence Clinton, that is now suspected to be a witch, went to Mr. Rogers' house, and told Mr. Rogers' maid that she might have some meat and some milk. And the [maid] said Rachel went into several rooms of the said house . . . And when she saw me come in, she, the said Rachel, went away, scolding and railing, calling me . . . "**hellhound**" and "**whoremasterly rogue**," and said I was **limb of the devil**. And she said she had rather see the devil than see me . . . (Samuel Ayers and Thomas Smith, tailor, can testify to the same language that Rachel used or called the said Knowlton.) And after this the said Rachel took up a stone and threw it toward me, and it fell short three or four yards off from me . . . and so came rolling to me, and just touched the toe of my shoe. And presently my was in a rage, as if the nail were held up by a pair of **pincers**. . . . And further the said Thomas Knowlton testified and saith that about three months ago my daughter Mary did wake and cried out in a dreadful manner that she was pricked of her side with pins, as she thought. Being asked who pricked her, she said she could not tell. And when she was out of her fits, I . . . asked whether she gave Rachel any pins, she said she gave Rachel about seven. After this she had one more fit of being pricked.*

What happened next . . .

Although Clinton was jailed for being a witch, Massachusetts Governor William Phipps put a stop to all witchcraft

deposition: a testimony taken under oath that is written down as an official record

hellhound: a mythical creature believed to guard the gates of hell

whoremasterly rogue: expression used to describe a person of lose moral character who will do anything for money

limb of the devil: expression used to accuse someone of being in partnership with the devil

pincers: tweezers

trials and executions before her sentence was carried out. She finally obtained her freedom in 1693 when the governor granted a general reprieve to prisoners being held as accused or convicted witches (see Chapter 4).

Did you know . . .

- The "afflicted girls" (Susannah Sheldon, Elizabeth Booth, Elizabeth Hubbard, Mary Warren, Mary Walcott, Sarah Churchill, Mercy Lewis, and **Ann Putnam, Jr.** [see biography and primary source entries]) who had accused and sent to death dozens of innocent people went so far as to accuse Lady Phipps (wife of Governor Phipps) of being a witch. One week later Governor Phipps halted all witchcraft hearings.

For Further Study

Demos, John Putnam. *Entertaining Satan: Witchcraft and teh Culture of Early New England.* New York: Oxford University Press, 1982.

Rice, Earle, Jr. *The Salem Witch Trials.* San Diego, California: Lucent Books, 1997.

Starkey, Marion L. *The Devil in Massachusetts: A Modern Enquiry into the Salem Witch Trials.* New York: Doubleday, 1989.

Cotton Mather

From *The Wonders of the Invisible World* (1693)

Reprinted in *American Literature: A Prentice Hall Anthology*, Volume 1 in 1991
Edited by Emory Elliott and others

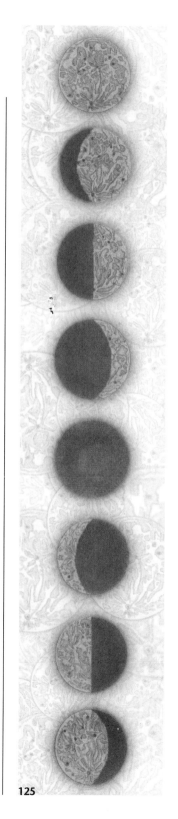

Cotton Mather (see biography and primary source entry with Ezekial Cheever) was a prominent minister in Boston, Massachusetts, who became closely involved in the Salem witch trials. Although he was not a trial judge, he worked in conjunction with his father, Increase Mather (see primary source entry), to root out witches who were doing the work of the devil in New England. Cotton Mather thought that witches were not possessed by spirits, but that they were agents of the devil. Modern historians have been mystified by Cotton Mather: although he was one of the foremost American intellectuals and scientists of the time, he was capable of deep superstition, even ignorance, in religious matters. According to Mather, witches had been sent as divine judgment against a sinful people. Therefore, witches—or sin—had to be destroyed before the Puritans could fulfill their destiny as "a people of God" in America ("once the Devil's territories").

In 1693 Mather wrote *The Wonders of the Invisible World,* in which he defended the Salem trials in lofty theological (religious) terms, with biblical references to support

The Wonders of the Invisible World:

Being an Account of the

TRYALS

OF

Several Witches,

Lately Executed in

NEW-ENGLAND:

And of several remarkable. Curiosities therein Occurring.

Together with,

I. Obfervations upon the Nature, the Number, and the Operations of the Devils.

II. A fhort Narrative of a late outrage committed by a knot of Witches in *Swede-Land*, very much refembling, and fo far explaining, that under which *New-England* has laboured.

III. Some Councels directing a due Improvement of the Terrible things lately done by the unufual and amazing Range of *Evil-Spirits* in *New-England*.

IV. A brief Difcourfe upon thofe *Temptations* which are the more ordinary Devices of Satan.

By *COTTON MATHER.*

Publifhed by the Special Command of his EXCELLENCY the Governour of the Province of the *Maffachufetts-Bay* in *New-England.*

Printed firft, at *Bofton* in *New-England*; and Reprinted at *London*, for *John Dunton*, at the *Raven* in the *Poultrey.* 1693.

his view of the Puritan mission in the New World. According to Mather, the devil was trying "all sorts of methods to overturn this poor plantation, the Puritan colony." Yet Mather saw this as a special challenge: once the Puritans were rid of the witches in their midst (had trodden "all the vultures of Hell" under their feet), God would bless them with eternal happiness ("halcyon days").

Things to remember when reading *The Wonders of the Invisible World:*

- Unlike his father (Increase Mather), in the beginning Cotton Mather rejected the concept of spectral evidence (proof of possession by spirits); instead, he regarded Salem as a battleground between the forces of good and evil.

- Like all Puritans, Mather believed that God had dispatched him on a special mission to the New World: his role was to root out evil and establish the "kingdom of God."

From The Wonders of the Invisible World

The New-Englanders are a people of God settled in those, which were once the Devil's territories; and it may easily be supposed that the Devil was exceedingly disturbed, when he perceived such a people here accomplishing the promise of old made unto our blessed **Jesus,** *That He should have the utmost parts of the earth for his possession. There was not a greater uproar among* **Ephesians,** *when the* **Gospel** *was first brought among them, than there was among the powers of the air (after whom those Ephesians walked) when first the silver trumpets of the Gospel here made the joyful sound. The Devil thus irritated immediately tried all sorts of methods to overturn this poor plantation: and so much of the church, as was fled into this wilderness, immediately found the serpent cast out of his mouth a flood for the carrying of it away. I believe that never were more satanical devices used for the unsettling of any people under the sun, than what have been employed for the* **extirpation** *of the vine which God has here planted, casting out the* **heathen,** *and preparing a room before it, and causing it to take deep root, and fill the land, so that it sent its boughs unto the Atlantic Sea eastward, and its branches unto the Connecticut River westward, and the hills were covered with the shadow thereof. But, all those attempts of Hell, have hitherto been abortive, many an* **Ebeneezer** *has been erected unto the praise of God, by his poor people here; and having obtained help from God, we continue to this day. Wherefore the Devil is now making one attempt more upon us; an attempt more difficult, more surprising, more*

Jesus: Jesus of Nazareth, founder of Christianity

Ephesians: people of Ephesus, in present-day Turkey, to whom Saint Paul preached

Gospel: the word of the Christian God

extirpation: the destruction of

heathen: an uncivilized or irreligious person

Ebeneezer: stone set up by Samuel in the Bible to commemorate victory over the Philistines

snarl'd with unintelligible circumstances than any that we have hith-
erto encountered; an attempt so critical, that if we get well through,
*we shall soon enjoy **halcyon** days with all the vultures of Hell trodden*
*under our feet. He has wanted his **incarnate** legions to **persecute** us,*
as the people of God have in the other hemispheres been persecuted:
he has therefore drawn forth his more spiritual ones to make an
attack upon us.

halcyon: happy

incarnate: in bodily form

persecute: to cause to suffer
because of belief

What happened next . . .

By September 1693 many intellectuals and ministers
started to question the use of spectral evidence in the witch
trials. The belief that accused witches were possessed by the
devil, rather than acting freely as a follower of the devil,
started to take hold. Once people started to feel that the
accused were really victims, the basis for the trials started to
crumble. Mather, who had originally been against the use of
spectral evidence but had pushed for the prosecution of some
of the accused solely on that charge, worked to distance himself from the shame of the outcome of more than a year of trials and executions.

In 1700 **Robert Calef** published *More Wonders of the*
Invisible World, a book mostly devoted to mocking Mather's
book (see biography and primary source entries). Although
Mather defended his views on witchcraft for the rest of his life,
he was mostly ignored. He is still considered to be at fault for
a great deal of the witchcraft hysteria.

Did you know . . .

- Although Cotton Mather was an extremely intelligent and
  well-educated man, he was passed over for the presidency
  of Harvard all his professional life. Bitter and angry for the
  slight, Mather assisted in the founding of Yale University,
  which to this day is one of Harvard's greatest rivals.

For Further Study

Demos, John Putnam. *Entertaining Satan: Witchcraft and the Culture of Early New England.* New York: Oxford University Press, 1982.

Discovery Online—A Village Possessed: A True Story of Witchcraft. http://www.discovery.com/stories/history/witches/witches.html (Accessed July 7, 2000).

Elliot, Emory, and others, eds. *American Literature: A Prentice Hall Anthology,* Volume 1. Englewood Cliffs, New Jersey: Prentice Hall, 1991.

Hansen, Chadwick. *Witchcraft at Salem.* New York: George Braziller, 1969.

Hill, Frances. *A Delusion of Satan: The Full Story of the Salem Witch Trials.* New York: Doubleday, 1995.

Rice, Earle, Jr. *The Salem Witch Trials.* San Diego, California: Lucent Books, 1997.

Starkey, Marion L. *The Devil in Massachusetts: A Modern Enquiry into the Salem Witch Trials.* New York: Doubleday, 1989.

Samuel Sewall

Diary Entries of Samuel Sewall

Apology of Samuel Sewall

**Both reprinted in *Early American Writing* in 1994
Edited by Giles Gunn**

Samuel Sewall (1652–1730; see biography entry) was a prominent Boston businessman who served on the panel of judges for the Salemwitch trials. He is best known today for his diary, which provides an eyewitness account of the internal workings of the procedings. The trials were conducted by a group of elite Puritan leaders who were convinced that they were following the will of God. Sewall was a member of that group. Selected diary entries from April, August, and September 1692—at the height of the trials—show that judges and other Puritan officials regularly consulted about strategy, and they were determined to obtain confessions from suspected witches. Yet they were also anxious to justify their decisions. For instance, interrogators piled stones on Giles Corey for nine days until he died because he would not admit to the charges against him. Sewall apparently needed to defend this act because he noted that Corey himself had crushed someone to death eighteen years earlier. As proof against Corey he cited spectral evidence: Corey's "specter" (spirit) appeared to **Ann Putnam, Jr.** the night before the execution and told her he had killed the man. Sewall took comfort in **Cotton Mather's** view

that the several convicted witches "all died by a righteous sentence." (See biography and primary source entries for both Putnam and Mather.) Sewall noted that some people thought George Burroughs (one of the executed men) was innocent, but he dismissed them as merely "unthinking persons." In the brief but dramatic description of the reprieve (the release from her death sentence) of Dorcas Hoar, Sewall indicated that the Puritans would call off an execution if a person confessed. Sewall later repented for his role in the trials.

Things to remember while reading the *Diary Entries of Samuel Sewall:*

- Sewall was actually an ordained minister, not a judge. However, at the time of the witch trials, people were chosen to sit on courts as judges based on their social standing and not on whether or not they had any legal training.

- Giles Corey was pressed to death because he contested the charges of witchcraft against him and refused to stand trial. Historians suggest that Corey must have known his case was hopeless, and therefore decided to defend the truth by refusing a trial.

- The witch trials were brought on by a mass hysteria that made many people actually believe that they were being haunted or possessed by evil.

From Diary Entries of Samuel Sewall

*April 11, 1692. Went to Salem, where, in the meeting-house, the persons accused of witchcraft were examined; was a very great assembly; 'twas awful to see how the **afflicted** persons were agitated. Mr. Noyes pray'd at the beginning, and Mr. Higginson concluded.*

*August 19, 1692. This day George Burroughs, John Willard, John Proctor, Martha Carrier and George Jacobs were **executed** at Salem, a very great number of spectators being present. Mr. Cotton Mather was there, Mr. Sims, Hale, Noyes, Chiever, &c. All of them said they were innocent, Carrier and all. Mr. Mather says they all died by a righteous sentence. Mr. Burroughs by his speech, prayer, **protestation** of his innocence, did much move unthinking persons, which occasions their speaking hardly concerning his being executed.*

*August 25. **Fast** at the old [First] Church, respecting the witchcraft, drought, &c.*

Monday, September 19, 1692. About noon, at Salem, Giles Corey was press'd to death for standing mute; much pains was used with him two days, one after another, by the Court and Capt. Gardner of Nantucket who had been of his acquaintance: but all in vain.

September 20. Now I hear from Salem that about 18 years ago, he [Giles Corey] was suspected to have stampd and press'd a man to death, but was cleared. Twas not remembered till Ann Putnam [Jr.] was told of it by said Corey's spectre the sabbath-day night before execution.

September 21. A petition is sent to town in behalf of Dorcas Hoar, who now confesses: accordingly an order is sent to the sheriff to for-

afflicted: distressed, suffering

executed: to put to death in compliance with a legal sentence

protestation: a solemn declaration

fast: going without eating food

bear her execution, notwithstanding her being in the warrant to die tomorrow. This is the first condemned person who has confess'd.

Thursday, September 22, 1692. William Stoughton, **Esqr.,** *John Hathorne, Esqr., Mr. Cotton Mather, and Capt. John Higginson, with my Brother . . . were at our house, speaking about publishing some Trials of the Witches.*

forbear: to hold back or abstain

Esqr.: esquire—used as a title of courtesy

What happened next?

As the witch-hunts continued into October 1692, the jails were continually filled with people accused of being witches and practicing witchcraft. However, by mid-October people seemed to start questioning whether the accused were witches, or whether they had just been "possessed" by the devil. Suddenly the courts were looking at the accused with more caution, as they believed a person possessed was not aware of what evil they were performing. Finally, after the publication of Increase Mather's speech "Cases of Conscience Concerning Evil Spirits Personating Men," which called into question the use of spectral evidence in the witchcraft trials, Massachusetts Governor William Phipps called an end to all witch trials.

As the Salem trials gained momentum and continued into 1693, the Puritan elite began expressing grave doubts about the witch-hunts. In addition to Increase Mather's changing his position on the use of spectral evidence, to condemn people, Increase's son Cotton also changed his mind, eventually supporting his father's view that the witch-hunts had been unjustified. Finally, in 1697, Massachusetts officials concluded that the trials had been a terrible mistake. The governor pardoned all condemned prisoners, and the legislature designated January 14 as a special day of atonement (expression of regret and request for forgiveness). By this time Samuel Sewall deeply regretted the role as judge he had played in the tragedy. Unlike the Mathers, Sewall had not been one of the main promoters of the trials; yet he had cooperated with those in power by sentencing and executing the accused witches. Sewall was so remorseful that he wrote an admission of error and guilt. Then on January 14, the day of atonement, he stood in front of the congregation in the Old South Church at Boston as the Reverend Samuel Willard read Sewall's statement aloud.

Samuel Sewall regretted having ordered the executions of hardworking, good people such as Giles Corey. *Reproduced by permission of Culver Pictures, Inc.*

Things to remember while reading *The Apology of Samuel Sewall:*

- The guilt and shame of the execution of the first accused witch (**Bridget Bishop**; see biography entry) led to the resignation of magistrate Nathaniel Saltonstall. Unable to be a part of the trials any longer, he left saying that the fits that a handful of Salem girls used as evidence of being "bewitched" and spectral evidence were not good sources for primary evidence. He was replaced by Johnathan Corwin.

- At the end of the trials, when the court of Oyer and Terminer was closed, Sewall was the only judge who felt enough shame for what had occurred that he apologized in front of the church congregation.

The Apology of Samuel Sewall

*Samuel Sewall, sensible of the **reiterated** strokes of God upon himself and his family; and being sensible, that as to the guilt contracted, upon the opening of the late Commission of **Oyer and Ter-***

reiterated: repeated

Oyer and Terminer: the court that conducted the witchcraft trials

benignity: kindness

sovereignty: supreme rule or excellence or an example of it

vouchsafe: to grant as a privilege or special favor

efficacious: having the power to produce a desired effect

*miner, he is, upon many accounts, more concerned than any that he knows of, desires to take the blame and shame of it, asking pardon of men, and especially desiring prayers that God, who has an unlimited authority, would pardon that sin and all his other sins; personal and relative: And according to his infinite **benignity**, and **sovereignty**, not visit the sin of him, or of any other, upon himself or any of his, nor upon the land: But that He [God] would powerfully defend him against all temptations to sin, for the future; and **vouchsafe** him the **efficacious**, saving conduct of his word and spirit.*

What happened next?

Sewall, broken and shamed for his part in the trials, worked to become more socially active in the later years of his life. He became a vocal advocate for the rights of the oppressed, including Native Americans and African slaves. He also set aside one day of fasting each year to atone for his involvement in the deaths of so many.

Did you know?

- Samuel Sewall wrote an abolitionist pamphlet called *The Selling of Joseph,* condemning the selling and trading of African slaves.

- Sewall was one of the first would-be Native American advocates who suggested placing tribes on reservations.

For Further Study

Discovery Online—A Village Possessed: A True Story of Witchcraft. http://www.discovery.com/stories/history/witches/witches.html (Accessed July 7, 2000).

Gunn, Giles, editor. *Early American Writing.* New York: Penguin Books, 1994.Hansen, Chadwick. *Witchcraft at Salem.* New York: George Braziller, 1969.

Hill, Frances. *A Delusion of Satan: The Full Story of the Salem Witch Trials.* New York: Doubleday, 1995.

Rice, Earle, Jr. *The Salem Witch Trials.* San Diego, California: Lucent Books, 1997.

Robert Calef

From More Wonders of the Invisible World (1697)

Reprinted in *American Literature: A Prentice Hall Anthology*, Volume 1 in 1991 Edited by Emory Elliott and others

Boston merchant Robert Calef (see biography entry) was one of the chief critics of the Salem witch trials. In 1697 he wrote *More Wonders of the Invisible World* in response to *Wonders of the Invisible World,* a justification of the trials written by **Cotton Mather** in 1693. Mather, in turn, had based his own evidence on works written by his father, Increase Mather (see Cotton Mather's biography entry and primary source entries for both). The Mathers had been largely responsible for encouraging the witch-hunts that began in the mid-1680s. Calef's book contained evidence that had not been presented either by the Mathers or at the trials—such as jurors' and judges' apologies, accusers' confessions to lying under oath— thus exposing the proceedings as a sham orchestrated by a small group of Puritan zealots. Calef published *More Wonders* in 1700, seven years after a reprieve had been granted to surviving accused and convicted prisoners, and after the Mathers themselves had expressed doubts about the trials.

The following excerpt from *More Wonders* is typical of Calef's approach in the book. Although he attacked the Mathers and trial officials, his real target was the Puritans' reliance

Robert Calef's book spoke of how Cotton Mather had betrayed his scientific knowledge by promoting the use of spectral evidence. He found the entire witch-hunt to be as uncivilized as the ones in Europe.

Reproduced by permission of the Gamma Liaison Netwrok.

on spectral evidence, the claim that a person's spirit (presumably taken over by the devil) committed an evil act. Calef questioned the use of spectral evidence as the entire basis of the trials. For instance, in the first paragraph below, he criticized Increase Mather's book *Cases of Conscience* for documenting the testimony of "bewitched" accusers, which could not be supported by visible evidence—even when the accusers were supposedly being bewitched in the courtroom and spectators could not see any changes in their appearance ("they did not stir from the bar"). In the next two paragraphs he berated the Puritans for their "unscriptual" belief in the devil. He pointed out that the Bible makes no mention of witchcraft, and therefore gives no basis for the existence of witches' pacts with the devil, nor for the trial of witches. Calef implied that if God had not created witches but humans were still claiming that witches existed, then God must not be in control of Nature. Calef concluded by saying that Mather was therefore engaging in "highly criminal" acts by encouraging the trials.

Things to remember while reading *More Wonders of the Invisible World:*

- *More Wonders* seems to have had an impact only on Increase and Cotton Mather, who spent the rest of their lives trying to redeem their reputations, which they claimed had been damaged by Calef. It was the Mathers that originally condemned the use of spectral evidence in witchcraft trials, but stood by while many people were found guilty of being witches based only on spectral evidence. In some cases, Cotton Mather even encouraged the use of spectral evidence.

- Although Calef's book had few readers in the early eighteenth century, it has remained an important document for modern historians because it provides a distinctly different Puritan voice from the trial era.

From More Wonders of the Invisible World

Mr. I. [Increase] Mather, in his Cases of Conscience, *tells of a **bewitched** eye, and that such can see more than others. They were certainly bewitched eyes, that could see as well shut as open, and that could see what never was; that could see the prisoners upon the **afflicted**, harming them, when those whose eyes were not bewitched could have sworn that they did not stir from the bar. The accusers are said to have suffered much by biting, and the prints of just such a set of teeth, as those they accused had, would be seen on their flesh; but such as had not such bewitched eyes have seen the accusers bite themselves, and then complain of the accused. It has been seen, when the accused, instead of having just such a set of teeth, has not had one in his head. They were such bewitched eyes, that could see the poisonous powder (brought by specters) and that could see in the ashes the print of the band, there invisibly heating the torment the pretended sufferers with, etc. . . . .*

*The way whereby these people are believed to arrive at a power to afflict their neighbors is by a compact with the Devil, and that they have a power to **commission** him to those evils. However, **irrational**, or*

bewitched: to have a spell cast over

afflicted: one in great distress

commission: having the power to order someone into service

irrational: does not make sense

unscriptural, such assertions are, yet they seem a necessary part of the faith of such as maintain the belief of such a sort of witches.

*As the Scriptures know nothing of a **covenanting** or **commissioning** witch, so reason cannot conceive how mortals should by their wickedness arrive at a power to commission angels, fallen angels, against their innocent neighbors. But the Scriptures are full in it, and the instances numerous, that the Almighty Divine Being has this **prerogative,** to make use of what instruments he pleaseth, in afflicting any, and **consequently** to commission devils: and though this word, commissioning, in the author's former books, might be thought to be **inadvertency,** yet now, after he hath been cautioned of it, still to persist in it seems highly criminal.*

What happened next . . .

More Wonders of the Invisible World contributed to an increased distrust of and dislike for Cotton Mather and his father, Increase Mather. Many people were already placing a great deal of the blame for the Salem hysteria with the Mathers, and Calef's book only made people mock and jeer them more. Increase Mather even went as far as to collect copies of Calef's book and have them burned publicly in Harvard Square, the central courtyard at Harvard College, but it made little impact. Although Cotton Mather defended his views on witchcraft for the rest of his life, he was mostly ignored. It is also believed that it is greatly due to this public ridicule that Cotton Mather was never appointed the presidency at Harvard, which he wanted dearly.

Did you know . . .

• Robert Calef wrote many books in his lifetime, but *More Wonders of the Invisible World* is the only one that is still actively reproduced today.

For Further Study

Elliot, Emory, and others, eds. *American Literature: A Prentice Hall Anthology,* Volume 1. Englewood Cliffs, New Jersey: Prentice Hall, 1991.

Rice, Earle, Jr. *The Salem Witch Trials.* San Diego, California: Lucent Books, 1997.

Ann Putnam, Jr.

The Apology of Ann Putnam, Jr. (1706)
Reprinted in *A Delusion of Satan: The Full Story of the Salem Witch Trials* **in 1995 Written by Frances Hill**

Many of the young girls who made accusations in the Salem witch trials apparently moved away from Salem when they became adults. Records do not indicate, however, what happened to Abigail Williams, Elizabeth Hubbard, Susannah Sheldon, or Mary Warren. The most detailed story found by historians is that of Ann Putnam, Jr. (see biography entry), who stayed in Salem Village for the rest of her life. Both of her parents died of an unknown infectious disease within months of one another in 1699, leaving Putnam to raise her nine younger siblings by herself. In 1706, at age twenty-seven, Putnam was admitted to membership in the Salem Village church. During the ceremony she made a public apology for her role in the imprisonment and execution of innocent people during the trials fourteen years earlier. The Reverend Joseph Green, who had replaced the banished **Samuel Parris** (see biography entry) as minister of the church, read Putnam's statement to a restless and embittered congregation, many of whom had taken part in both sides of the conflict. Putnam admitted that innocent people had been wrongfully accused, but she claimed to have acted not out of anger or malice but instead out of a "great delusion of Satan." In other words, she herself had been bewitched by the devil.

Ann Putnam, Jr. had accused many people of practicing witchcraft; eventually some were executed.
Reproduced by permission of Corbis.

Putnam opened her apology by saying that she had been a victim of "that sad and humbling providence that befell my father's family in the year about '92": a child at the time of the trials, she was used as "an instrument for the accusing of several persons of a grievous crime." She was referring the fact that the Putnams—her father, Thomas Putnam, and his brothers and their families—had been the main source of witchcraft accusations against certain Salem residents. At the end of the apology Putnam said she was particularly sorry for being "a chief instrument of accusing of Goodwife Nurse and her two sisters."

Things to remember while reading *The Apology of Ann Putnam, Jr.:*

- Ann Putnam, Sr. (Ann Putnam, Jr.'s mother) believed in the occult, and convinced Ann at an early age that there was an evil, hidden world of demons, devils, and witches.

- Ann Putnam, Sr. also played a principle part in accusing people of witchcraft.

- Historians have concluded that one of the motivating factors of the trials was the boundary dispute the Putnams had been waging with their neighbors for over fifty years; the trials were thus a convenient way for them to seek revenge on their enemies (see Chapter 4). The Putnams' main rivals were the Towne family, and three Towne sisters—Rebecca Nurse, Elizabeth Procter, and Sarah Cloyce—were all tried and condemned to death. (Nurse was hanged; Procter and Cloyce were not executed.)

The Apology of Ann Putnam, Jr.

*I desire to be **humbled** before God for that sad and humbling **providence** that befell my father's family in the year about '92; that I, then being in my childhood, should, by such a providence of God, be made an instrument for the accusing of several persons of a **grievous** crime, whereby their lives were taken away from them, whom now I have just grounds and good reason to believe they were innocent persons; and that it was a great **delusion** of Satan that deceived me in that sad time, whereby I justly fear I have been instrumental, with others, though **ignorantly** and **unwittingly**, to bring myself and this land the guilt of innocent blood; though what was said or done by me against any person I can truly and uprightly say, before God and man, I did it not out of any anger, **malice**, or ill-will to any person, for I had no such thing against one of them; but what I did was ignorantly, being deluded by Satan. And particularly, as I was a chief instrument of accusing of Goodwife [Rebecca] Nurse and her two sisters [Elizabeth Procter and Sarah Cloyce], I desire to lie in the dust, and to be humbled for it, in that I was a cause, with others, of so sad a **calamity** to them and their families; for which I desire to lie in the dust, and earnestly beg forgiveness of God, and from all those unto whom I have given just cause of sorrow and offence, whose relations were taken away or accused.*

humbled: shamed

providence: the control and protection of God

grievous: causing grief

delusion: deception

ignorantly: unknowingly

unwittingly: without meaning to

malice: harm

calamity: a disaster or something that causes distress

What happened next . . .

After her apology, Ann, Jr. was allowed to rejoin the membership of the church. Her fate was not to be improved, however, as she remained unmarried and was in poor health for the rest of her life. She died in 1716, at the age of thirty-seven.

Did you know . . .

- Today there are no laws having to do with witchcraft left on the books in Massachusetts. In 1992, however, the Massachusetts House of Representatives decided to pass a legal resolution restoring the good names of people who had been condemned as witches but had never been officially forgiven.

For Further Study

Demos, John Putnam. *Entertaining Satan: Witchcraft and the Culture of Early New England.* New York: Oxford University Press, 1982.

Hansen, Chadwick. *Witchcraft at Salem.* New York: George Braziller, 1969.

Hill, Frances. *A Delusion of Satan: The Full Story of the Salem Witch Trials.* New York: Doubleday, 1995.

Kallen, Stuart A. *The Salem Witch Trials.* San Diego, California: Lucent Books, 1999.

Rice, Earle, Jr. *The Salem Witch Trials.* San Diego, California: Lucent Books, 1997.

Nathaniel Hawthorne

From *"Young Goodman Brown"* (1835)

Reprinted in *The American Tradition in Literature* **in 1974**
Edited by Sculley Bradley and others

"Young Goodman Brown," a short story by nineteenth-century American fiction writer Nathaniel Hawthorne (see biography entry), was based on the history of his Puritan ancestors and the New England of his own day. Hawthorne documented Puritan hypocrisy in many of his stories (which he called "tales"), such as *The Scarlet Letter* (1850) and *The House of Seven Gables* (1851). One of his best-known tales is "Young Goodman Brown"(1835), which tells the story of a young, devout Puritan named Goodman Brown. One evening he leaves his wife, Faith, at home in Salem while he takes a walk in the woods. Disappointed to learn that others have been on the path before him, he happens upon a witches' sabbath, where he is shocked to see his own wife. Sick at heart, he returns to Salem the next morning. He has been changed from a happy and youthful man to a confused and bitter man, who goes to his grave convinced that the world is full of sinners.

The following excerpt is the conclusion of "Young Goodman Brown." It opens just after Brown has seen Faith, and he is still upset and shocked from the experience. He cannot decide whether it was a dream or reality. (Hawthorne frequently used actual historical figures in his stories; notice that here he mentions Goodie Cloyse, who was Sarah Cloyce, one of the condemned witches in the Salem trials.)

Things to remember while reading "Young Goodman Brown":

- Nathaniel Hawthorne was born over one hundred years after the end of the Salem, Massachusetts, witch craze.

- Hawthorne's ancestors had an especially strong impact on his imagination and on his name (Nathaniel added the "w" to his last name in order to separate himself from the evil acts of his ancestors). William Hathorne settled in Boston in the 1630s and was involved in the persecution of Quakers (members of the Society of Friends). William's son John was one of the chief judges in the Salem witchcraft trials (see Chapters 3 and 4).

From "Young Goodman Brown"

"Faith! Faith!" cried the husband [Goodman Brown], "look up to heaven, and resist the wicked one."

*Whether Faith obeyed he knew not. Hardly had he spoken when he found himself amid calm night and **solitude**, listening to a roar of the wind which died heavily away through the forest. He staggered against the rock, and felt it chill and damp; while a hanging twig, that had been all on fire, besprinkled his cheek with the coldest dew.*

*The next morning young Goodman Brown came slowly into the street of Salem village, staring around him like a bewildered man. The good old minister was taking a walk along the graveyard to get an appetite for breakfast and **meditate** his **sermon**, and **bestowed** a blessing, as he passed, on Goodman Brown. He shrank from the **venerable** saint as if to avoid **anathema**. Old Deacon Gookin was at **domestic** worship, and the holy words of his prayer were heard through the open window. "What God doth the wizard pray to?"*

*quoth Goodman Brown. Goody Cloyse [Sarah Cloyce], that excellent old Christian, stood in the early sunshine at her own **lattice, catechizing** a little girl who had brought her a pint of morning's milk. Goodman Brown snatched away the child as from the grasp of the **fiend** himself. Turning the corner by the meeting house, he spied the head of Faith, with the pink ribbons, gazing anxiously forth, and bursting into such joy at sight of him that she skipped along the street and almost kissed her husband before the whole village. But Goodman Brown looked sternly and sadly into her face and passed on without a greeting.*

Had Goodman Brown fallen asleep in the forest and only dreamed a wild dream of a witch-meeting?

*Be it so if you will; but, alas! It was a dream of evil **omen** for young Goodman Brown. A stern, a sad, a darkly meditative, a distrustful, if not desperate man did he become from the night of that fearful dream. On the Sabbath day, when the congregation were singing a holy **psalm**, he could not listen because an **anthem** of sin rushed loudly upon his ear and drowned all the blessed strain. When the minister spoke from the **pulpit** with power and **fervid eloquence**, and, with his hand on the open Bible, of the sacred truths of our religion, and of saint-like lives and triumphant deaths, and of future bliss or misery unutterable, then did Goodman Brown turn pale, dreading lest the roof should thunder down upon the gray **blasphemer** and his hearers. Often, awaking suddenly at midnight, he shrank from the bosom of Faith; and at morning or eventide, when the family knelt down at prayer, he scowled and muttered to himself, and gazed sternly at his wife, and turned away. And when he had lived long, and was borne to his grave a hoary corpse, followed by Faith, an aged woman, and children and grandchildren, a goodly procession, besides neighbors not a few, they carved no hopeful verse upon his tombstone, for his dying hour was gloom.*

lattice: fence

catechizing: giving religious instruction

fiend: Satan

omen: an occurrence believed to predict a future event

psalm: (pronounced *SALM*) a sacred song or poem used in worship

anthem: a long song or hymn

pulpit: an elevated platform used in preaching or conducting worship service

fervid: passionate

eloquence: expressiveness

blasphemer: one who seems not to care about rules and morals

What happened next . . .

Hawthorne went on to write *The Scarlet Letter,* which is the most widely read of his literary works. In 1852 Hawthorne was appointed overseas U.S. consul (official government representative) at Liverpool, England, where he served from 1853 to 1857. Upon returning to the United States in 1860, he and his wife settled into their first real home at Concord. After a mysterious illness, and refusing to take medical attention, in 1864 Hawthorne died in his sleep. Before his death he had started writing four new books, none of which was ever completed.

Did you know . . .
- Nathaniel Hawthorne believed that what one generation of a family did came back to haunt later generations. He believed it so strongly that it even showed up in one of his books, *The House of the Seven Gables* (which also happens to be a house in what used to be Salem Village): "the wrong-doing of one generation lives into the successive ones."

For Further Study

Bradley, Sculley, and others, ed. *The American Tradition in Literature*. New York: Gossett and Dunlap, 1974.

Hawthorne, Nathaniel. *Young Goodman Brown*. New York: Oxford University Press, 1999.

The Hawthorne Treasury: Complete Novels and Selected Tales of Nathaniel Hawthorne. New York: Modern Library, 1999.

Carl L. Weschke

"The Principles of Wiccan Belief"
Reprinted in *Drawing Down the Moon* in 1979
Written by Margot Adler

Neo-Paganism is a term applied to a number of related movements that have attempted to revive ancient polytheistic (belief in more than one god) religions of Europe and the Middle East during the twentieth century. This term is customarily used in place of such words as "pagan" and "witch" because of negative associations with the witch-hunts that took place during the Middle Ages in Europe and during the seventeenth century in New England. Yet many Neo-Paganists call themselves witches, or Wiccans, and they meet in covens (the ancient word for groups of witches). While covens differ in structure and ritual, they share a tendency to worship nature as a way to renew connections between human beings and the universe.

When Neo-Paganism began to emerge in the 1960s, most covens met independently and often secretly, creating a sense of mystery. There were complex reasons for this separateness and lack of openness, such as the wish to avoid being misunderstood as worshipers of Satan or to preserve the validity of rituals. By the early 1970s, however, a split had taken place among the diverse groups: some insisted on maintaining strict codes of secrecy and would not reveal the names of mem-

bers of their groups; others wanted to announce themselves and share their ideas with people in the mainstream society. Yet most groups accepted the central Wiccan creed, "An ye harm none, do what ye will"; that is, people are free to act as long as they do not harm others.

In an attempt to unify the Wiccan movement, the Council of American Witches was organized and met in Minneapolis, Minnesota, in April 1973 to draft "The Principles of Wiccan Belief." The statement was written by Carl L. Weschke, director of the council and owner of Llewelyn Publishing, which printed witchcraft documents.

Things to remember while reading "The Principles of Wiccan Belief":

- Wiccans practice what is considered "white" magic, or good magic. They do not seek to harm or hurt anyone or anything.

- It is not a part of Wiccan belief to worship the devil or practice evil.

- Wicca was officially recognized in the United States as a non-profit religious sect in 1975, two years after this was written.

"The Principles of Wiccan Belief"

The Council of American Witches finds it necessary to define modern Witchcraft in terms of the American experience and needs.

*We are not bound by traditions from other times and other cultures, and owe no **allegiance** to any person or power greater than the Divinity **manifest** through our own being.*

*As American Witches we welcome and respect all **Life Affirming** teachings and traditions, and seek to learn from all and to share our learning within our Council.*

*It is in this spirit of welcome and cooperation that we adopt these few principles of Wiccan belief. In seeking to be **inclusive**, we do not wish to open ourselves to the destruction of our group by those self-serving power trips, or to philosophies and practices **contradictory** to those principles. In seeking to exclude those whose ways are contradictory to ours, we do not want to deny participation with us to any who are sincerely interested in our knowledge and beliefs, regardless of race, color, sex, age, national or cultural origins or sexual **preference**. . . .*

*We practice Rites to **attune** ourselves with the natural rhythm of life forces marked by Phases of the Moon and the Seasonal Quarters and Cross Quarters.*

*We conceive of the Creative Power in the Universe as manifesting through **polarity**—as **masculine** and **feminine**—and that this same Creative Power lives in all people, and functions through the **interaction** of the masculine and feminine. We value neither above the other, knowing each to be supporting of the other. . . .*

We see religion, magick, and wisdom-in-living as being united in the way one views the world and lives within it—a worldview and philosophy-of-life which we identify as Witchcraft, the Wiccan Way.

allegiance: devotion

manifest: obvious

life affirming: something that is positive

inclusive: to include

contradictory: expressing the opposite

preference: choice

attune: adjust

polarity: opposite sides

masculine: to have male traits

feminine: to have female traits

interaction: to affect one another

Calling oneself "Witch" does not make a witch—but neither does **heredity** *itself, or the collecting of titles, degrees and* **initiations**. *A Witch seeks to control the forces within him/herself that make life possible in order to live wisely and well, without harm to others, and in harmony with Nature. . . .*

We do not accept the concept of "absolute evil," nor do we worship any entity known as "Satan" or "The Devil". . . . We do not seek power through the suffering of others, nor do we accept the concept that personal benefit can only be derived by denial to another.

We acknowledge that we seek within Nature for that which is **contributory** *to our health and well-being.*

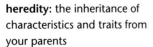

heredity: the inheritance of characteristics and traits from your parents

initiations: memberships to groups

contributory: contributes, adds to

What happened next . . .

The Council of America Witches disbanded in 1974. The following year the Covenant of the Goddess (CoG) was formed to incorporate hundreds of separate Wiccan covens and was officially recognized as a church in the United States. The CoG is the largest Wiccan organization, representing a variety of belief systems and practices. At the end of the twentieth century Wicca was the eighth largest religion in the United States, ranking with Christianity, Buddhism, Islam, and other established faiths.

Did you know . . .

- According to the Institute for the Study of American Religion, Neo-Paganism is the fastest growing religion in the United States.

- Wiccan spiritual practices and rituals coincide with the phases of the moon, the solstices (the beginnings of Summer and Winter) and equinoxes (the beginnings of Spring and Fall) and traditional celebrations such as May Day and Halloween.

 The Wiccan Code of Ethics

- Witches must follow the *Wiccan Rede*, "An' ye harm none, do what ye will."

- No fees can be charged for initiations (admission) or initiate (new member) training.

- "Reasonable fees" may be charged for services that earn a living.

- The autonomy (self-governing) and sovereignty (independence) of other witches and covens must be respected.

- Witches should be mindful of both the unity and diversity of their religion.

For Further Study

Adler, Margot. *Drawing Down the Moon: Witches, Druids, Goddess-Worshippers, and Other Pagans in America Today.* Boston, Massachusetts: Beacon Press, 1986.

Barstow, Anne Llewellyn. *Witchcraze: A New History of the European Witch Hunts.* San Francisco, California: Harper, 1999.

Buckland, Ray. *Witchcraft From the Inside.* St. Paul, Minnesota: Llewelynn Publications, 1995.

Guiley, Rosemary Ellen. *The Encyclopedia of Witches and Witchcraft,* 2nd ed. New York: Checkmark Books, 1999.

Biographies

Bridget Bishop

Born: c. 1640
England
Died: June 10, 1692
Salem, Massachusetts

Tavern owner and accused witch

Bridget Bishop was the first person to be put to death during the Salem witch trials of 1692 and 1693. She was accused of practicing witchcraft by practically everyone who had known her: her neighbors, husband, and employees all came forward to speak of being put under a spell by her, thus building the strongest case in all the Salem trials. No one defended Bishop. The townsfolk became convinced that witches were working in their midst, and fear quickly swept across the region. As a result twenty innocent people were condemned to die.

Known for flashy outfits

Little is known about Bridget Bishop's early life aside from her marriages. The public record of Bishop's life begins in England in about 1660 when she was around the age of twenty. She was married for the first time at this point, and she was soon widowed (her spouse died during their marriage) for unknown reasons. Bishop arrived in New England shortly thereafter and was briefly married to Goodman Wasselbee, who died under mysterious circumstances. She then married a

It was thought that the devil would give to witches dolls or puppets to carry out evil deeds on different people.

Reproduced by permission of Pennsylvania State University.

widower, Thomas Oliver of Salem Town, in 1666, but this relationship ended in divorce amid accusations of witchcraft brought against her. In 1687 she married Edward Bishop, her fourth husband, a successful lawyer who would also eventually testify against her in court.

Bishop was known for her unusual sense of fashion and for her friendliness with men. She owned two taverns, one in Salem Village and the other in Salem Town. (Salem Village, near the Atlantic coast, was a bustling, densely populated city. Salem Town, farther inland, was in a poorer, predominately agricultural area.) She got along well with her patrons, especially younger men, as she allowed them to play games like shuffleboard until the early hours of the morning. Bishop's tolerance for this merriment soon aroused suspicion and anger from her neighbors. The fact that she dressed in bright, suggestive clothing also damaged her reputation. Bishop was famous for an outfit that consisted of a black cap and a red bodice (corset, upper part of a dress) looped with laces of various colors, which she had dyed to order by the local fabric dyer Samuel Shattuck. She was also known for her strong temper, an unacceptable quality in women of that day.

Long accused of being a witch

The first witchcraft charges against Bishop were brought in 1670 by her third husband, Thomas Oliver. Testimony from the trial has not survived but it is known that Bishop's clergyman, John Hale, convinced the community to let her go free in the hope that she would mend her ways. In 1687 she was again accused of being a witch and acquitted (found not guilty). These new charges came from several different people. One was a complaint that she had caused the death of a neighbor. Other neighbors agreed that after arguments with Bishop they had fallen ill or been tormented by her specter (spirit). Though she was not imprisoned on these charges they later resurfaced during the Salem trials.

On April 18, 1692, Bishop was summoned to be examined in a preliminary hearing at Salem Village. "Bewitched" teenage girls in the village had named her as a witch and held her responsible for their violent fits and spectral hauntings. During the first hearing the girls put on a great show, copying Bishop's every gesture as she sat on the witness stand. If she rolled her eyes, they would do the same. When she shifted her position they would shift too, but in a manner that attracted greater attention from the audience. Although Bishop denied practicing witchcraft, she stood hardly any chance of passing through this initial questioning phase and she was swiftly sent to prison to await trial.

Samuel Shattuck and the Tiny Outfits

Fabric dyer Samuel Shattuck testified against Bridget Bishop with his own peculiar evidence at the Salem trials. For years he had dyed lace and clothing for her and he spoke of mysteriously small pieces she frequently brought to him to be dyed: "sundry pieces of lace, some of which were so short that [he] could not judge them fit for any use," as quoted by Chadwick Hansen in *Witchcraft at Salem.* The implication was clear: Bishop had asked Shattuck to dye outfits too small to be worn by a human being, but suitably sized for a doll or replica of a person. This was interpreted as evidence that Bishop was a witch. Popular folklore held that a witch used dolls to cast spells on a person, and to make the spells work effectively the witch would clothe a doll in the same general colors and style worn by the victim.

Empowered by his confession, Shattuck went on to speak of an incident years earlier when his son had fallen into violent and strange fits. A stranger had suggested taking the presumably bewitched child to visit Bishop, as it was believed that blood from a witch's face was an effective way of breaking a spell. Shattuck agreed and paid the man to take his son to Bishop's tavern under the pretense of buying cider. Once inside the man was to scratch her face and draw some blood in order to stop the boy's illness. When they reached the tavern, however, Bishop refused to sell them any cider and instead scratched the boy's face before chasing the stranger off with a spade. The boy fell extremely ill after this episode and local doctors declared that he was indeed bewitched.

Shattuck's testimony, coupled with that of the men who had found the puppets in the walls of Bishop's house, made clear that Bishop was a practicing witch who had attempted to cause harm to her fellow townspeople. While other testimony was mainly circumstantial and likely caused by the fear her reputation provoked, the town dyer confirmed suspicions that Bishop's practices had been deliberate (on purpose) and malicious (with a desire to harm).

Evidence against Bishop came in many forms and from a wide variety of sources, thus indicating to modern historians that in all likelihood she was an actual practicing witch. This sets her apart from most of the other accused people who were innocent victims of local rivalries and fears. Bishop's case also fueled the public's imagination and made matters worse for others accused, as it presented tangible (able to be treated as fact) evidence of her guilt as a visible practicing witch. The most damaging evidence came from two men who had broken down a wall in her house while they were doing some repairs. As they were working the men discovered dolls with pins stuck in them, an apparently common form of witchcraft in which a person would inflict harm on others by making models of their bodies and harming them by injuring the puppet. Although nobody had seen Bishop put the dolls into the wall, the evidence was strongly against her and she herself was unable to summon a reasonable defense.

Bishop's specter haunts neighbors

Several people came forward during the trial to complain of Bishop's specter haunting them, both in her image and in the shape of bizarre animals. A man named Richard Coman testified that eight years earlier he had experienced a series of frightening hauntings. Over a period of several nights he, his wife, and two friends who were staying at the Coman home had been haunted by Bishop and two other unfamiliar specters. According to Coman's testimony, she:

> came in her red paragon bodice and the rest of her clothing which she then usually did wear. . . . She came and lay upon my breast or body and so oppressed me that I could not speak nor stir, no not so much as to awake my wife, although I endeavored much to do it. The next night they all appeared again in like manner and the said Bishop took hold of me by the throat and almost hauled me out of bed. (From Chadwick Hansen, *Witchcraft at Salem*, p. 67

The haunting apparently ended when one of Coman's friends called out the name of God in the room, but the damage was done.

Apparently, Bishop's reputation struck fear even into those who had never come into conflict with her. They too came forward with hysterical charges. A man named Samuel Gray described an incident that had occurred fourteen years earlier, when he awoke to an apparition (spirit) similar to the one described by Conan although he was not acquainted with Bishop. Gray claimed Bishop's specter had entered his bedroom and caused his sleeping child to go into fits. The child died several weeks later. When Gray finally came across Bishop

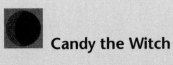

Candy the Witch

During Bridget Bishop's trial, a case similar to her own helped seal charges against her and confirmed the existence of other practicing witches in the Salem area.

A black slave named Candy, who came from Barbados, an island in the Caribbean, was examined on evidence provided by afflicted teenage girls who said she had bewitched them. Candy explained that she had not been a witch in Barbados but instead had learned everything she knew from local women who brought her "The Book," the witches' handbook, and instructed her. When asked how she was trained to hurt people, Candy said she had used puppets to inflict harm. When she was asked to bring these puppets to court she went out and fetched her collection of knotted rags. Some of these rags had grass and cheese inside of them, and all were held together with knots to form a figurine that slightly resembled a person. Historical documents show that when Candy brought the dolls into the courtroom the accusing girls fell into hysterical fits. She was forced to eat some of the cheese inside one of her bundles and apparently "that night was burned in her flesh" as a result, according to records collected in *Witchcraft in Salem*.

Other tests were run on the rag dolls to determine their power. One doll was put under water and instantly its targeted victim experienced the sensation of drowning or choking. Another of the female victims apparently tried to run to the river to drown herself as soon as her puppet was immersed, but was held back by neighbors. This brief episode helped confirm the case against Bishop while also leaving a record for contemporary historians regarding the faith people had in these supposed methods of witchcraft. They strongly believed that certain people could inflict damage through magic, a fact that affected all social interactions, particularly conflicts.

in person he claimed he recognized her immediately (again by her clothing) as the specter that had invaded his house.

One of Bishop's neighbors, John Louder, recalled a similar experience in which she came to him in the night and strangled him repeatedly while sitting on him. He claimed he actually confronted Bishop about this event while picking fruit the next day and he immediately became ill. While recovering at home he experienced a vivid confrontation with a black pig that vanished whenever he tried to kick it away but then reap-

peared again and again until he said the name of God. Louder claimed the beast left him alone after that but that it shook all of the apples off his trees on its way out of his house. While this testimony was sufficient on its own, Bishop made the error of claiming she had never met John Louder, despite the fact that they were neighbors.

Bishop's fate is sealed

Finally, Bishop's own husband testified against her in court, claiming he had witnessed her acts of witchcraft for many years as well as noting her absence from church each Sunday. (To miss attending church services on Sunday, the Christian day of worship, was punishable in some communities.) During her trial no evidence in her favor was allowed into the court. While she was being held in jail Bishop apparently spoke with Mary Warren, another accused witch, who believed that the teenage girls were making things up about her. Bishop tried to use this in her own defense in court, implying that the girls were simply being malicious, but the authorities would not allow these remarks to be put into court records. Bishop's son would have testified on her behalf but he was arrested during her trial for trying to beat the truth about the false accusations out of John Indian (husband of **Tituba**, another woman accused of being a witch, and who accused others of being witches; see biography entry) and for threatening to beat the accusing girls for playing games with the town. Even John Hale, the minister who had saved Bishop during previous charges of witchcraft, was now fully convinced she was guilty.

Bishop was declared guilty on June 4, 1692, and sentenced to be hanged. Although an old Massachusetts law forbade hanging, it was struck down on June 8: the courts applied an even earlier colonial law stating that witchcraft was a crime punishable by death. Thus, on June 10, Bishop was led through the streets of town bound to a cart as crowds of onlookers thronged around the first hanging of the Salem trials. On Gallows Hill she was hanged by High Sheriff George Cowan off the branch of a large oak tree in what was to be the first of twenty executions.

For Further Reading

Discovery Online—A Village Possessed: A True Story of Witchcraft. [Online] http://www.discovery.com/stories/history/witches/witches.html (Accessed July 7, 2000).

Hansen, Chadwick. *Witchcraft at Salem.* New York: George Braziller, 1969.

Hill, Frances. *A Delusion of Satan: The Full Story of the Salem Witch Trials.* New York: Doubleday, 1995.

Kallen, Stuart A. *The Salem Witch Trials.* San Diego, California: Lucent Books, 1999.

Ogram's 17th Century New England with special emphasis on The Salem Witchcraft Trials of 1692. [Online] http://www.ogram.org/17thc/index. shtml (Accessed July 7, 2000).

Rice, Earle, Jr. *The Salem Witch Trials.* San Diego, California: Lucent Books, 1997.

The Salem Witch Museum. [Online] http://www.salemwitchmuseum.com/ (Accessed July 7, 2000).

Starkey, Marion L. *The Devil in Massachusetts: A Modern Enquiry into the Salem Witch Trials.* New York: Doubleday, 1989.

Robert Calef

Born: 1648
England
Died: 1719
Roxbury, Massachusetts

Civil servant, merchant, and writer

Robert Calef's most significant contribution to American history was criticism of various aspects of the Salem witch trials of 1692–93. Through the written and spoken word he provided one of the few voices of dissent (disagreement) during a turbulent time. Some historians credit him with ending the trials, while others believe he exploited aspects of the events for his own benefit.

Collects evidence against trial officials

Robert Calef was born in England and arrived in Boston, Massachusetts, in 1688 when he was about forty-eight years old. In Boston he held various jobs, such as cloth merchant, constable, tax collector, and assessor. Known around the city as a witty man, Calef frequently engaged in lively discussions at coffee houses. He had a wide circle of influential friends and was respected for his intelligence. It is not known whether he was married or had children, as most existing records document only his writing and public life. Until his

UDOVICI LAVATERI.
Theologi eximii,
DE
PECTRIS, LEMURIBUS, VARII
PRÆSAGITIONIBUS,
Tractatus vere aureus.

LUGDUNI BATAV:
pud Henricum Verbief
Anno M.DC.LIX.

Many books were being written about witchcraft, but Calef's was one of few that spoke about specific people having to do with the trials, such as Cotton Mather. *Reproduced by permission of the Corbis Corporation (Bellevue).*

death in 1719 he was an active, respected member of the Municipal Board (a city governing agency).

Shortly before the end of the Salem trials in 1693, Calef began collecting letters and testimony from people who had been involved in or were affected by the proceedings. Having watched events from a distance, he stepped closer to examine specific details and wrote at length about his impressions. His accounts give modern historians a different point of view on the trials because he was not afraid to speak his mind. Although he was considered a pious (very religious) Puritan (a strict branch of Christianity), he was determined to tell the truth about the injustices committed in the name of Christianity.

Calef was most critical of the use of spectral evidence as the primary means of determining the guilt of accused witches. Through spectral evidence, an accuser could claim he or she saw the accused's spirit committing an evil deed. Attacking the courts for permitting such unprovable evidence in the trials, Calef suggested that the officials themselves had been tricked by the devil. He felt that the devil, as the "father of lies," had effectively turned New Englanders against one another by using illusion and fear as his primary agents and thus destroying communities from within. At this time few people except the accused witches and their loved ones were speaking out against the trials, so Calef's allegations were controversial and upsetting.

Calef and the Mathers

On September 13, 1696, three years after the trials had ended, Calef was alerted to another possible witch-hunt. Thomas Brattle, a local merchant and critic of the Salem trials, informed him that Boston minister **Cotton Mather** (see biography and primary source entries) was once again "curing witches." Mather had taken a young girl named Margaret Rule into his home in an attempt to treat her for possession by evil spirits. At the time of the witch trials, Mather was widely known for his attempts to cure "bewitched" (cast under a spell) women through months of fasting (eating little or no food) and prayer, keeping detailed written records for future reference. He had supposedly rid quite a few women of evil spirits prior to treating Rule.

Margaret Rule "Bewitches" the Mathers

Margaret Rule's stay in Cotton Mather's home in 1696, three years after the Salem witch trials ended, attracted considerable attention due to the wild nature of her "possession." She frequently entered into violent fits similar to those the afflicted teenage girls had experienced during the Salem trials (convulsions, feeling as though she were being pinched, etc.). The memory of this time was still fresh in the Massachusetts colony so Calef, fearing another witch-hunt, decided to witness Mather's methods himself. What he observed was not a person possessed by evil spirits but rather a young woman who craved the attention of men. She could be soothed in her fits only by the "laying on of hands." Only men, however, could calm Rule, who (according to Calef) implored Mather and his father Increase Mather to rub her face and naked belly. According to records cited in *The Devil in Massachusetts: A Modern Enquiry into the Salem Witch Trials*, when a woman attempted to soothe her in the same manner she retorted, "Don't you meddle with me!" One evening Calef witnessed her telling all women to leave the room because she preferred the company of men. He also noted that Rule told Cotton Mather certain local women were witches, a matter he chose to keep secret.

Fearing that this young woman could cause another outbreak of witch-hunt hysteria, Calef felt the Mathers were encouraging her craving for male attention because they too were enjoying the experience. Calef kept the notes and letters he had written during this period, planning to publish them in a book as a preventive measure in stopping future false accusations. Ironically, just before Rule was "cured" she had one last episode, during which she named the demon who was afflicting her. Reportedly she named her haunter as none other than Cotton Mather himself.

"Another Brand Plucked From the Fire"

Calef's observations of events in the Mather home and his correspondences with Mather on the topic of witch curings would eventually turn into a major source of tension between the two men. Calef's critique of Mather culminated in *More Wonders of the Invisible World or Another Brand Plucked From the Fire* (1697; see primary source entry), which some scholars consider to be a valuable contribution to American history. Calef wrote the book in response to Mather's *Wonders*

At the time that Calef
wrote *More Wonders of the
Invisible World* matters
had reached true hysteria
in Salem Village.
*Reproduced by permission of
the Corbis Corporation
(Bellevue).*

of the Invisible World (1693), in which Mather had defended
the Salem trials. Calef's book is a voluminous collection of letters and testimony from judges and witnesses, as well apologies from jurors and others involved in the trials. Not only
had Mather conveniently left these documents out of his
book but, without Mather's permission, Calef also included
incriminating letters written by Mather. The letters demon-
strate Mather's defensiveness about his role in the trials and
give vivid details about the case of Margaret Rule that hinted
that her behavior was sexual in nature, rather than the evil
affliction that she was believed to have had and for which she
had been treated.

More Wonders of the Invisible World was not officially
published until 1700, and then it was released in England.
Nevertheless, copies of the book reached the colonies, causing
a major blow to Mather's reputation. In 1700 Mather wrote in
his diary:

Though I had often cried unto the Lord, that the cup of this man's [Calef's] abominable bundle of lies, written on purpose, with a quill under a special energy and management of Satan, to damnify my precious opportunities of glorifying my Lord Jesus Christ, might pass from me; yet, in this point the Lord had denied my request; the book is printed, and the impression is this week arrived here. (From Frances Hill, *A Delusion of Satan*)

Mather was so outraged that he had Calef arrested for libel (a printed statement that wrongly damages a person's reputuation), claiming he falsified supposed eyewitness accounts of what had transpired with Rule. The case never actually went to court, but Mather wrote Calef a series of desperate letters begging him to clear his name. He was particularly concerned about the passages that implied a sexual relationship between him and Rule, insisting he had never touched her. Calef gave in, admitting that when he wrote that Mather had "rubbed [Rule's] stomach, her breast not covered with the bedclothes," he had merely meant that her body was partially exposed. Yet it was still a damaging statement, and Calef's portrayal of the incident haunted Mather until his death.

Provides documentation of trials

Increase Mather, Cotton's father, collected copies of Calef's book and had them burned publicly in Harvard Square, the central courtyard at Harvard College, in Cambridge, Massachusetts. This act did not diminish the book's popularity, however, and Cotton Mather was immortalized as one of the main villains in the Salem trials. In an effort to defend Mather's reputation, several of his parishioners published a rebuttal to Calef's work titled *Some Few Remarks upon a Scandalous Book* (1701), but it failed to redeem Mather.

Calef enjoyed the notoriety he had gained from his book. It is likely that he exaggerated some facts to catch the attention of his readers and to cast doubt on the motivations of Puritan leaders in handling the witchcraft problem. Many modern historians insist that Mather actually played only a small role in the trials, and his crime was the same as that committed by most people at the time: he had surrendered to a genuine fear of evil. Yet he did not help his own situation because he showed no remorse for the deaths of the twenty innocent people executed for witchcraft.

In spite of possibly distorting the facts, Calef made a contribution to the historical documentation of the trials by collecting a wide array of letters and testimonials into one complete volume. The real target of his critique was not the Mathers but the very basis of the trials: the notion that the devil could possess people who would then torment others by appearing to them as specters. Calef was one of the few critics who dared to attack the widely held belief system around witchcraft and to ask people to question their own participation in the trials.

For Further Reading

Hansen, Chadwick. *Witchcraft at Salem.* New York: George Braziller, 1969.

Hill, Frances. *A Delusion of Satan: The Full Story of the Salem Witch Trials.* New York: Doubleday, 1995.

Kallen, Stuart A. *The Salem Witch Trials.* San Diego, California: Lucent Books, 1999.

Rice, Earle, Jr. *The Salem Witch Trials.* San Diego, California: Lucent Books, 1997.

The Salem Witch Museum. [Online] http://www.salemwitchmuseum.com/ (Accessed July 7, 2000).

Starkey, Marion L. *The Devil in Massachusetts: A Modern Enquiry into the Salem Witch Trials.* New York: Doubleday, 1989.

Wilson, Lori Lee. *The Salem Witch Trials.* New York: Lerner, 1997.

Rachel Clinton

Born: c. 1629
Suffolk County, England
Died: c. 1695
Ipswich, Massachusetts

Homemaker, care giver, and accused witch

Rachel Clinton was one of many people accused in the New England witch-hunts who regained her freedom in 1693 after a court-ordered reprieve. Her story shows how a formerly wealthy and respected citizen could be reduced to poverty after being wrongly accused of practicing witchcraft. It also one of the few documented accounts of witch-hunts elsewhere in Massachusetts prior to the Salem trials of 1692–93.

The Haffield family fortune

Rachel Clinton was born Rachel Haffield, the daughter of Richard and Martha Haffield, in Suffolk County, England, in 1629. Her father had a considerable amount of wealth and property but married below his social station when he took Martha as his second wife. Martha came from a poor family and apparently resented the higher social standing of Richard's first wife, and let it be known it in many ways, including showing great animosity toward the two children from his previous marriage. This economic discrepancy (difference) was destined to become a curse once the family arrived in the colonies.

Rachel Clinton was first stripped of all her worldly goods and her good name, before finally being accused of being a witch. *Reproduced by permission of the Corbis Corporation (Bellevue).*

In 1635 the Haffields sailed for New England aboard the ship *The Planter* with their five daughters, one of whom was six-year-old Rachel. They settled in the town of Ipswich, near Salem, Massachusetts, where they became one of the wealthiest families in the region. When Richard suddenly died in 1639 he left a will in which he ordered that his estate be divided evenly among his wife and five daughters. Yet the will triggered years of quarrels and bitterness in the family, particularly in regard to the children of his first marriage. Martha received the bulk of the inheritance as well as the power to distribute other funds to the children. Strife within the family was met with equal tension in the community, which resented the flaunting of so much excess in a time of widespread poverty. Court records of 1639 show, however, that the eldest daughter Ruth was formally charged with dressing too extravagantly. The case was dismissed because of the Haffields's great wealth.

Town officials step in

Martha never remarried after Richard's death. One by one the daughters married and started their own homes. As Martha's mental health slowly deteriorated, Rachel took over management of the estate with the full permission of her mother. Nevertheless, this arrangement was overlooked by local magistrates (legal officials) who felt a need to take matters into their own hands. In 1666 they decided to hold a court session to discuss what should be done about the widow Haffield's declining mental health and, more precisely, who should be in charge of her money. The officials granted partial power of attorney (right to handle financial and legal affairs) to Thomas White, husband of Rachel's half-sister Ruth, with the agreement that he would use part of the money from the estate to pay for the care of Martha. Initially he was given only the power to collect rents from properties owned by the Haffields. Several months later, however, White was given sole authority over Martha's affairs. According to John Putnam Demos in *Entertaining Satan: Witchcraft and the Culture of Early New England*, his role was "to be as a guardian to her . . . and to receive and recover her estates." Two months after taking over full power of attorney, White brought a court case against Ipswich landowner Robert Cross.

Buys future husband's freedom

In 1665 Cross, who owned a fairly sizable estate, had employed newcomer Lawrence Clinton as an indentured servant (someone contracted to an employer for a specified length of time in exchange for free passage from Europe to the colonies). Almost immediately Clinton became involved with Rachel Haffield, who was single and wanted to be married. At this time, an indentured servant could be released from a contract only by paying the employer the balance of money due on the contract. Thirty-six year old Rachel and twenty-two year old Lawrence could not marry immediately because of this one stipulation, so Cross agreed to free Lawrence for the price of twenty-one pounds (an amount of British money). Rachel was still informally in charge of her mother's estate and cash, so she easily obtained the funds to free Clinton from his obligation. A year later her brother-in-law Thomas

White took over the Haffield estate, and he decided to hold Cross accountable for the money because he claimed it had been illegally obtained. White charged Rachel with stealing the money from her mentally ill mother and pointed an accusing finger at Cross, whom he felt had taken advantage of Rachel's desire to wed.

Although it was common knowledge in Ipswich that Rachel had her mother's permission to handle the family money, there was never any formal written agreement. When the court granted power to White it robbed Rachel of any legal standing and made her look like a criminal for using the funds to free her future husband. In the court trial over the twenty-one pounds the jury decided in favor of White. This decision was reversed just a few months later, so Cross set up an elaborate scheme in hopes of reaping further profit from the case. He urged his former servant to marry Rachel and gain full access to her family's estate. He then told Rachel lies about Clinton's wealth in hopes of speeding up the wedding. According to *Entertaining Satan: Witchcraft and the Culture of Early New England* court records indicate Rachel felt used and cheated: Cross "told me a thousand lies more to delude me, so as to be married to him [Clinton] and to cause me to put money into his hands. Further, this deponent sayeth that in case the money now in controversy were taken from him again, then he would sell me and my husband Clinton for servants."

This time the jury found in favor of Cross, who was given back his twenty-one pounds. White let the case drop and focused his attention on selling off parts of Rachel's land, including the cottage where she had lived with her mother. He forced Martha to move in with him and his wife, leaving Rachel with nothing. In March 1668, almost immediately after the move, Martha died and the controversy over her holdings reached an even more intense level. The family farm was valued at about 300 pounds, and her own personal property was estimated to be worth about 50 pounds. White tried to seize everything and then attempted to collect a guardianship fee from the family, at the rate of 22 pounds per year, for taking care of Martha. He also added court costs involved in his case against Cross as well as expenses for Martha's funeral to his demands.

Rachel ruined

When Martha wrote a will six years prior to her death, she was still deemed to be of sound mind. In the will she specified that Rachel was to be in charge of the Haffield farm and other properties on the condition that she share the income generated by rents with her half-sisters Ruth and Martha. When they were granted only ten shillings apiece, the sisters sued for their share, which they had not yet received since their father's death; they lost their court case. During the struggle White passed away and the courts granted everything to his wife Ruth. Thus, almost thirty years after Richard's death, Rachel was left completely penniless while Ruth got the bulk of the estate to herself.

After Ruth gained control of the family wealth, Rachel was left homeless and penniless. She was even reduced to begging from her neighbors. She appealed to the community for assistance, claiming that her husband had abandoned her financially and emotionally from the beginning of their marriage when it was apparent she was not going to inherit the estate. Lawrence Clinton had a reputation for having relationships with other women and was charged in court both for adultery (a sexual relationship between a married person and someone who is not the person's spouse) and attempted rape. Although the courts ordered him to pay support to his wife, in 1671 Rachel went back to court to complain that he had not yet paid her any money. In the meantime Lawrence had fathered a child out of wedlock with a woman named Mary Greeley while carrying on an affair with another, Mary Wooden, for which he was publicly whipped. Humiliated and alone, Rachel begged the courts for a divorce but they refused to grant it. Instead they pressured Lawrence for back payment, which he would never provide. Rachel's case was not helped by the fact that she had admitted to having affairs with two men, for which she was also publicly whipped. At last, in 1681, the courts took pity on her and granted her a divorce. By this time Lawrence was already remarried and had fathered six children with various women.

Accused of witchcraft

During her later years Clinton was poor and completely alienated from the Ipswich community. Her lofty beginnings as a member of one of the area's wealthiest family had long before set the stage for resentment. When she plummeted into poverty and despair her neighbors ignored her sudden neediness and neglect at the hands of her husband and family. Viewed as an outcast and a burden, over time Clinton became a perfect target for accusations of witchcraft. Although records do not show the specific events leading up to formal charges, it is clear that her former Ipswich neighbors rallied against her (see *Witchcraft 1687: The Deposition of Thomas Knowlton against Rachel Clinton* in the Primary Sources section). Claiming she had a long-standing reputation of practicing witchcraft, they described bizarre events that had allegedly occurred as a result of her power. For instance, a woman named Mary Fuller, who had been her next door neighbor, stated that she had had an argument with Clinton and as a result a neighbor girl had died. Though it was later revealed that the girl had merely been sleeping, the community agreed that Clinton was capable of causing this kind of incident. In another instance, according to *Entertaining Satan*, a local man, Thomas Boreman, said in court that a wealthy woman had accused Clinton of "hunching [people] with her elbows" in church. He also claimed that one night strange animals crossed his path and then vanished into thin air as soon as he thought of Rachel Clinton. Other neighbors testified that on several occasions Clinton had cursed them and invoked the devil's name. They also contended it was common knowledge that she was a witch. Another man, William Baker, testified that ten years before the trial a massive quantity of beer had vanished from a vat without any apparent signs of a leak or theft. That same day he had been in a heated argument with Clinton and was sure she was responsible for the disappearance of the beer. Other witnesses testified against her with similar complaints.

In late 1692 Clinton was arrested as a suspected witch and was held in jail for many months until Massachusetts Governor William Phipps (1651–1695) granted the general reprieve to all prisoners in May 1693. She died about two years later with no property, no relationship with her sisters, and no ties to any members of the community. The exact date of Clinton's death remains unclear, but on January 7, 1695, the small hut she lived in on Hog Island off the coast of Ipswich was granted to Ruth White.

For Further Reading

Demos, John Putnam. *Entertaining Satan: Witchcraft and the Culture of Early New England.* New York: Oxford University Press, 1982.

Ogram's 17th Century New England with special emphasis on The Salem Witchcraft Trials of 1692. [Online] http://www.orgram.org/17thc/index.shtml (Accessed July 7, 2000).

Nathaniel Hawthorne

Born: July 4, 1804
Salem, Massachusetts
Died: May 19, 1864
Plymouth, New Hampshire

Writer and descendant of John Hathorne,
chief magistrate in the Salem trials

Although American author Nathaniel Hawthorne was born more than a hundred years after the Salem witch trials, he was profoundly affected by the Puritans' persecution of innocent people during the New England witch-hunts. Hawthorne was a direct descendant of the Hathornes, one of the founding families of the Massachusetts colony, and his ancestor John Hathorne was the chief magistrate in the trials that led to the deaths of twenty people. Haunted by his Puritan past, Hawthorne explored the issue of sin in such works as "Young Goodman Brown" (1835; see primary source entry), *The Scarlet Letter* (1850), and *The House of Seven Gables* (1851), which have become American literary classics.

The "haunted chamber"

Nathaniel Hawthorne's father was a sea captain who died of yellow fever in 1808, leaving his wife and three children dependent on relatives. Nathaniel, the only son, spent his early years in Salem, Massachusetts, and at a country home in Maine. Immobilized by a leg injury for a long period of time,

Nathaniel Hawthorne, one of the greatest American authors, was ashamed of the role his ancestor John Hathorne played in the Salem witch trials.

he developed an interest in reading and contemplation (the act of thinking or meditating about something thoughtfully). Although he was often isolated, he had a pleasant childhood, adored by his mother and two sisters and supported by relatives as he grew into adulthood. In 1821 Hawthorne's prosperous uncles, the Mannings, sent him to Bowdoin College, where fellow students were poet Henry Wadsworth Longfellow; future U.S. president Franklin Pierce; and Horatio Bridge, who would later finance one of Hawthorne's publications. After graduating from Bowdoin in 1825, Hawthorne returned to Salem and lived with his mother for twelve years. He spent most of his time alone in what he called a "haunted chamber," developing his skills as a writer and discovering the themes that later became the trademarks of his works. In 1838 he met Sophia Peabody, to whom he confided, "If ever I should have a biographer, he ought to make great mention of this chamber in my memoirs, because so much of my lonely youth was wasted here, and here my mind and character were formed," as quoted in the *Encyclopedia of World Biography*.

Hawthorne and Peabody were soon engaged, and he credited her with bringing him out into the world again. Although he had published several stories, which he called tales, his writing did not provide sufficient income to support a future wife and family. In 1839 he took a job measuring salt and coal at the Boston Custom House, where he stayed until 1841, when he invested $1000 in Brook Farm Community, a well-known commune (a group that jointly owns property and shares daily chores). Hawthorne thought Brook Farm would provide an economical home for himself and Peabody, but he soon became disenchanted with the experiment in communal living. After their marriage in 1842 the couple moved to Old Manse of Concord, a similar community whose residents included essayist Ralph Waldo Emerson, writer Henry David Thoreau, and clergyman Ellery Channing. The Hawthornes stayed at Old Manse until 1846, when Nathaniel took a position as surveyor at the Salem Custom House. He was dismissed in January 1849 as a result of local political conflicts.

Hawthorne was discouraged about losing his job, but his wife urged him to devote himself to writing. Within two years he had produced *The Scarlet Letter* and *The House of Seven Gables*. Immediate acclaim from critics and other writers gave him the motivation to continue publishing his work. In 1852, when his old friend Pierce was elected president, Hawthorne was appointed overseas U.S. consul (official government representative) at Liverpool, England, where he served from 1853 to 1857. In 1857 the family moved from England to Italy, living mainly in Florence and Rome. Upon returning to the United States in 1860, they settled into their first real home at Concord, New Hampshire. Despite a lifetime of vigor and few illnesses, Hawthorne's health went into a mysterious decline. Refusing medical attention, he died in his sleep on May 19, 1864, while on an expedition with Pierce. Before his death he had started four other books, none of which was completed.

Hawthorne and the Salem trials

Hawthorne was deeply affected by the legacy of his ancestors and the shameful association of his family with the Salem witch trials. He was especially troubled by the deeds of John Hathorne. Hawthorne reportedly added a "w" to the fam-

The Legacy of John Hathorne

Nathaniel Hawthorne's first Puritan ancestor was major William Hathorne, who settled in Boston, Massachusetts, in the 1630s before moving on to Salem as one of the founders of the town. In the introduction to *The Scarlet Letter* Hawthorne described his ancestor as "a grave, bearded, sable-cloaked and steeple-crowned progenitor—who came so early with his Bible and sword . . . and had all the Puritanical traits, both good and evil." William expressed his Puritan fervor by persecuting Quakers (members of the Society of Friends). His son John earned an even more infamous reputation for persecution as an unrepentant magistrate during the Salem witch trials of 1692–93.

Born in 1641, John inherited the privileges of an elite Salem family. During his lifetime he was a prosperous landowner, merchant, and judge. In 1684 he was appointed chief magistrate of the local court system, a position that gave him the principal role in questioning defendants during the witch trials eight years later. Transcriptions of the trials show that Hathorne presumed all accused persons to be guilty until proven innocent, so he used aggressive tactics to force them into making confessions. As an advocate of spectral (spirit) evidence, he accepted fantastical testimony as fact; therefore, the only way a suspect could avoid execution was to confess to the crime of witchcraft. Hathorne exploited the theatrical nature of the trials by calling upon supposedly bewitched (cast under a spell) girls as witnesses to confront accused witches in court, a move that doomed several people when the girls fell into fits. His bullying led many innocent people to Gallows Hill. Despite his role in the ordeal, Hathorne never expressed any remorse. Unlike his colleague **Samuel Sewall** (see biography and primary source entries), for instance, Hathorne did not make a public apology. Hathorne lived to an advanced age, enjoying great wealth and the respect of the community. This contradiction and Hathorne's involvement in the trials later haunted Nathaniel Hawthorne, providing the reason for the theme of inherited guilt in the author's works.

ily name in order to distinguish it from the Hathornes. This was not the only way he was affected, as his life in Salem also profoundly haunted him. Hawthorne's main literary theme was the inheritance of guilt. He felt strongly that the sins of one generation were passed on to the next generation and would play themselves out in a cycle of mischief and tragedy in small ways. From the actions of his ancestors Hawthorne thus developed the concept of an ancestral curse. In his tales he sought to emphasize the importance of the heart and the potential calamity of over-reliance on rational thinking (ideas based on reason), which leads to destructive intellectual pride.

Hawthorne's works

Hawthorne is widely regarded as the father of the American novel, a form of literature in which characters and plot are developed in a series of interrelated events. In his first published story, "The Hollow of the Three Hills" (1830), he explored guilt and sin and included a witch in his plot. Many of his other stories addressed these same themes, often incorporating witches or an encounter with the occult (conjuring of supernatural forces). In "Young Goodman Brown" (see primary source entry) an upright Puritan man becomes permanently disillusioned with the world after he sees his wife participating in a witches' Sabbath in the forest.

The Scarlet Letter is the most widely read of Hawthorne's works. Set in seventeenth-century Salem, the novel explores the issues of forbidden pleasure and sin. Puritan officials have forced the main character, Hester Prynne, to wear a red letter "A" as a sign that she committed adultery (had sexual relations with a man who was not her husband) after she had a baby daughter out of wedlock (without being married). Hester's struggle becomes even more painful when her husband, who has taken the false name of Roger Chillingworth, returns to Salem after an absence of several years. Learning that Hester's lover is a Puritan minister named Arthur Dimmesdale, he forces Dimmesdale to make a public confession. As the story unfolds, Hawthorne shows that Hester's surrender to passion is less troubling than the sins committed by the Puritans, who are represented by Chillingsworth and Dimmesdale. For instance, Chillingsworth is self-righteous and vindictive, while Dimmesdale is tortured by guilt and shame. Hester is eventually able to rise above adversity because she is true to the natural human spirit, but the two men ruin their lives by accepting repressive Puritan moral codes.

Literary scholars note that *The Scarlet Letter* and Hawthorne's other tales continue to appeal to modern readers because the author vividly depicted the era of the witch-hunts and the Salem trials. Yet his work also transcends the troubling legacy of America's Puritan past by providing an imaginative testing ground for the human struggle with the forces of evil.

For Further Reading

Encyclopedia of World Biography, Gale, 1998.

Erlich, Gloria. *Family Themes and Hawthorne's Fiction: The Tenacious Web.* New Brunswick, New Jersey: Rutgers University Press, 1986.

The Hawthorne Treasury: Complete Novels and Selected Tales of Nathaniel Hawthorne. New York: Modern Library, 1999.

Miller, Edwin Haviland. *Salem Is My Dwelling Place: A Life of Nathaniel Hawthorne.* Iowa City, Iowa: University of Iowa Press, 1991.

The Scarlet Letter. Boston: WBGH, 1998. Available on videocassette recording.

Cotton Mather

Born: 1663
Boston, Massachusetts
Died: 1728
Boston, Massachusetts

Clergyman, scientist, and writer

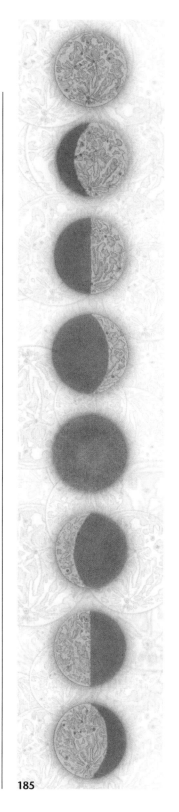

Puritan minister Cotton Mather was instrumental in escalating the witch-hunts in New England during the late
1600s. Along with his father, Increase Mather (1639–1723; see
primary source entry), who was also a prominent minister, he
published works providing evidence that witchcraft was being
practiced in Massachusetts communities. In 1693, after the
start of the Salem trials, Cotton Mather wrote *The Wonders of
the Invisible World,* in which he claimed that the devil was testing Puritans by bringing witches into their midst (see *The Wonders of the Invisible World* in the Primary Sources section). He
advocated (supported) waging a holy war against the forces of
evil by tracking down and eliminating witches. Yet Mather's
involvement in the trials continues to intrigue modern historians: although he was one of the great colonial American the-
ologians (reliogious scholar) and readily accepted such superstitions as the belief in witchcraft, he was also a leading
scientist. Mather and inventor Benjamin Franklin (1706–1790)
were the only colonial Americans to be elected to the Royal
Society of London, a prestigious scientific organization in England. Reconciling this aspect of his life with his religious views,

Mather advocated the study of science as a means of teaching about God. A well-informed amateur physician (one who has no formal medical training), Mather was at the forefront of promoting medical advances such as smallpox inoculation. His book *The Angel of Bethesda* (1722), a catalog of common ailments and their remedies, made significant contributions to colonial American medicine. A man of extreme contradictions, Mather had a life filled with disappointment and anguish.

Must fulfill family expectations

Cotton Mather was born in Boston, Massachusetts, in 1663, into a third generation of prominent Puritans. His father, Increase Mather, was an historian and prominent Boston clergyman and his grandfather, Richard Mather (1596–1669), was a famous Puritan minister. His mother, Maria Cotton Mather, was the daughter of John Cotton (1584–1652), an equally esteemed Puritan minister. Such an impressive family background placed considerable pressure on Mather as a young boy. He was expected to become a successful theologian like his father and grandfathers, and he set about fulfilling these high expectations. By the time he was a teenager he had mastered Latin, Greek, and other ancient languages. He had also learned how to deliver formal sermons (religious speeches). When Mather was fifteen he graduated from Harvard College in Cambridge, Massachusetts, and three years later he earned a master's degree from that institution. In 1685, when he was twenty-two, he was ordained (officially appointed by the church) as his father's colleague in the ministry at the prestigious Second Church in Boston. The following year Mather married Abigail Phillips.

Caught between religion and science

Soon Mather was a prominent member of the New England elite (powerful and influential class). At the same time he found himself involved in a period of profound religious and social change. Although he and his father were preaching the strict Puritanism introduced by the founding fathers of the Massachusetts colony, Mather realized the world was changing. New scientific ideas were rapidly reaching the American colonies from Europe, and many of these theories undermined the traditional teachings of Christianity. For instance, Christians believed that God created and

Increase Mather

Increase Mather, the father of Cotton Mather, was an historian and prominent Boston clergyman. He was also a leader in the scientific community. Mather adopted the new ideas of such European scientists as Francis Bacon (1561–1626) and Robert Hooke (1635–1703). He even incorporated scientific theories into his sermons. For instance, he tried to combat superstition by giving realistic explanations about comets and the nature of the universe. Newton's Comet of 1680 in particular inspired his interest in astronomy (the study of stars and planets). Mather organized the Philosophical Club of Boston in 1683; one of the members was twenty-year-old Cotton Mather.

In 1684 Increase Mather compiled *Remarkable Providences*, a collection of "proofs" of witchcraft. Eight years later he actively supported the witch trials in Salem, Massachusetts. By 1693, however, he had changed his mind, calling the witch-hunts a mistake in his book *Cases of Conscience Concerning Evil Spirits*. This work was instrumental in bringing the executions to an end. Mather served as president of Harvard College from 1685 until 1701.

Cotton Mather Witnesses Witchcraft Trials

Cotton Mather approved of the witchcraft trials held at Salem, Massachusetts, in 1692–1693, during which twenty people were executed. He published *Wonders of the Invisible World* (1693), defending the trials as being necessary in order to rid the colony of the influence of the devil. An excerpt from the "The Trial of Martha Carrier," a chapter in Mather's book, describes a typical case that came before the Salem court:

> At the Court of Oyer and Terminer [to hear and determine], Held by Adjournment at Salem, August 2, 1692
>
> I. Martha Carrier was indicted [brought to trial] for the bewitching certain persons, according to the form usual in such cases, pleading not guilty, to her indictment; there were first brought in a considerable number of the bewitched persons; who not only made the court sensible [aware] of an horrid witchcraft committed upon them, but also deposed [reported] that it was Martha Carrier, or her shape, that grievously tormented them by biting, pricking, pinching and choking of them. It was further deposed that while this Carrier was on her examination before the magistrates [judges], the poor people were so tortured that every one expected their death upon the very spot, but that upon the binding of Carrier they were eased. Moreover the look of Carrier then laid the afflicted people for dead; and her touch, if her eye at the same time were off them, raised them again: which things were also now seen upon her trial. And it was testified that upon the mention of some having their necks twisted almost round, by the shape of this Carrier, she replied, "It's no matter though their necks had been twisted quite off.
>
> II. Before the trial of this prisoner, several of her own children had frankly and fully confessed not only that they were witches themselves, but that their mother had made them so. This confession they made with great shows of repentance, and with much demonstration of truth. They related place, time, occasion; they gave an account of journeys, meetings and mischiefs by them performed, and were very credible in what they said. Nevertheless, this evidence was not produced against the prisoner at the bar [in court], inasmuch as there was other evidence enough to proceed upon. . . . After recording the testimony of numerous witnesses, Mather attached this note: Memorandum. This rampant hag, Martha Carrier, was the person of whom the confessions of the witches, and of her own children among the rest, agreed that the Devil had promised her she should be Queen of Heb [Queen of Hebrews]. (From Emory Elliot, and others, editors, *American Literature: A Prentice Hall Anthology*, p. 190.)

Mather later reversed his position and supported the view that the witch-hunts had been unjustified.

controlled the universe, whereas scientists were arguing that man could learn about the world by observing and studying nature itself. In fact, a divine creator seemed to have no place in scientific analysis.

Throughout his life Mather continued to preach traditional Christian principals. In the spirit of the Puritan fathers, he warned his congregations that God would punish unrepentant (not regretful) sinners. Mather claimed that God spoke to him in thunderstorms and appeared to him in the form of angels. Like his father, Mather approved of the witchcraft trials and executions held in Salem. When he published *Wonders of the Invisible World* in 1693, he defended the trials as being necessary to rid the colony of the influence of the devil. Mather later reversed his position and—again like his father—supported the view that the witch-hunts had been unjustified.

Pursues science with religion

Despite his success as a minister, Mather felt a strong pull toward science. Consequently, for forty years he struggled to make a connection between two apparently opposite world views. He firmly believed in the literal truth of the Bible (the holy book of the Christian faith), and he never doubted that God controlled world affairs. Nevertheless, when he was in his thirties he became one of the leading scientists of the early eighteenth century. In an effort to reconcile religion with science, he asserted that the world was created by God and understood through scientific study.

Mather's first publication was an analysis of the validity of the story of Noah's Ark. (According to the Old Testament, the first part of the Bible, Noah was a Jewish patriarch, or one of the original leaders of the Jews. He built a boat in which he, his family, and living creatures of every kind survived a flood that destroyed the rest of the world.) His masterpiece, *Magnalia Christi Americana*, a religious history of New England, appeared in 1702. Admitted to the Royal Society in 1713, he studied the work of such European scientists as Robert Boyle (1627–1691) and Isaac Newton (1642–1727). Mather published his views about the connection between religion and science in *The Christian Philosopher* (1721). In this work he argued that everything in the universe has a reason and a purpose. According to

The Wonders of the Invisible World.

OBSERVATIONS

As well *Historical* as *Theological,* upon the NATURE, th' NUMBER, and the OPERATIONS of the

DEVILS.

Accompany'd with,

I. Some Accounts of the Grievous Molestations, by DÆMONS and WITCHCRAFTS, which have lately annoy'd the Countrey; and the Trials of some eminent *Malefactors* Executed upon occasion thereof: with several Remarkable *Curiosities* therein occurring.

II. Some Counsils, Directing a due Improvement of the terrible things, lately done, by the Unusual & Amazing Range of EVIL SPIRITS, in Our Neighbourhood: & the methods to prevent the *Wrongs* which those *Evil Angels* may intend against all sorts of people among us. especially in Accusations of the Innocent.

III. Some Conjectures upon the great EVENTS, likely to befall, the WORLD in General, and NEW ENGLAND in Particular; as also upon the Advances of the TIME, when we shall see BETTER DAYES.

IV. A short Narrative of a late Outrage committed by a knot of WITCHES in *Swedeland,* very much Resembling, and so far Explaining, *That* under which our parts of *America* have laboured!

V. THE DEVIL DISCOVERED: In a Brief Discourse upon those TEMPTATIONS, which are the more Ordinary *Devices* of the Wicked One.

By **Cotton Mather.**

Boston Printed by *Benj. Harris* for *Sam. Phillips.* 1693.

Mather, the natural world glorifies the wisdom of God, who with perfect efficiency made only necessary things. By the end of his life Mather had published more than four hundred books and sermons. Numerous other works remained in manuscript (unpublished) form upon his death.

Encourages smallpox inoculation

During this time Mather also pursued his wide-ranging scientific interests. He wrote about fossils, astronomy, mathematics, zoology (the study of animals), entomology (a branch of zoology that deals with insects), ornithology (a branch of zoology dealing with birds), and botany (the study of plants). Like other clergymen, he studied and practiced medicine as an amateur. In his autobiography he explained that his attraction to medicine came about as a result of his own hypochondria (fear of illnesses). When he was a teenager he had an intense curiosity about medical literature. Devouring book after book, he eventually began to imagine that he himself had the symptoms of the diseases he was reading about. Over the years Mather became an authority on the causes and cures of mental illness, measles, scurvy (a disease caused by lack of vitamin C), fevers, and smallpox. In fact, in 1721 he was the foremost advocate of smallpox inoculation in America. (Smallpox is a highly contagious, often fatal viral disease that produces skin sores on the body. Inoculation is the introduction of the disease-causing agent into the body in order to create an immunity, or resistance.) Mather possibly promoted this new technique because of the terrible toll the disease had taken in his own life: two of his fifteen children and one of his three wives had died from smallpox.

Writes medical manual

In 1722 Mather wrote *The Angel of Bethesda,* a detailed study of the prevention and cure of common illnesses. Arguing that disease is the result of sin, he found a direct connection between the mind and the body. He also discussed techniques of psychotherapy (treatment of mental illness). Another important feature of the work was Mather's explanation of microorgasims (germs) as the cause of disease, a theory then being debated in Europe but not yet well known in America. Mather also kept a diary (published in 1911, 1912, and 1976), which ultimately expanded to seventeen volumes. The diary reveals the extent of Mather's anguish and profound disappointment in life.

Experiences setbacks and tragedy

Despite his achievements, Mather was constantly experiencing setbacks and tragedy. After the death of his first wife, Abigail, with whom he had a happy marriage, he wed Elizabeth Clark Hubbard in 1703. He and Elizabeth were happy together, but she too died at a young age. Mather's third marriage, to Lydia Lee George, was disastrous: Lydia reportedly ruined him financially before she went insane. With his three wives Mather had fifteen children, but only two survived at the time of his death. Neither of them was capable of carrying on the intellectual tradition of three previous generations of Mathers. For instance, his son Increase—named for Mather's father—preferred to spend his time in pubs (bars) instead of preparing for the ministry. Yet Cotton Mather was even more disappointed in himself. When he was not chosen to succeed his father as president of Harvard College, he concluded that he was a failure because he had not carried on the Mather tradition.

For Further Reading

Elliot, Emory, and others, eds. *American Literature: A Prentice-Hall Anthology*. Englewood Cliffs, New Jersey: Prentice Hall, 1991.

Levin, David. *Cotton Mather: The Young Life of the Lord's Remembrancer, 1663–1703*. Cambridge, Mass.: Harvard University Press, 1978.

Silverman, Kenneth. *The Life and Times of Cotton Mather*. New York: Harper & Row, 1984.

Wendell, Barrett. *Cotton Mather*. New York: Chelsea House, 1980.

Samuel Parris

Born: 1653
London, England
Died: 1720
Boston, Massachusetts

Minister of Salem Village church

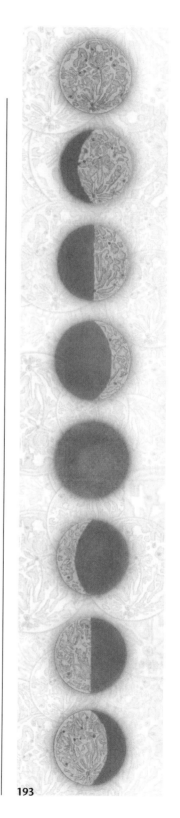

Samuel Parris was the minister of the church in Salem Village during the witch trials in 1692–93. A controversial figure since his arrival in the community several years earlier, he actively encouraged the witch-hunts, which had started in his own household when his daughter and niece lapsed into unexplained fits. Parris used his position to damage the lives and reputations of innocent people, most of whom were members of his own congregation. Despite efforts to remove him from his post after the trials were over, he managed to remain as pastor until he was finally forced to leave Salem five years later. Although he issued an apology for his role in the witch trials, he continued to blame the devil for stirring up trouble among good Christians.

Enters the troubled world of Salem Village

Little is known about Samuel Parris's early life in England. Historians do know, however, that at some point during adolescence he moved with his family to Barbados, an island in the West Indies, where his father owned a successful sugar trading company. Parris was sent to Harvard College to study theology (religion), but he never completed his degree. When his father died in 1678 he moved back to Barbados to take over the family business, and two years later he married Elizabeth Elridge. Parris's efforts to run the company were plagued with bad luck from the outset. At one point a hurricane wrecked the warehouses, and the consistently low sugar prices steadily reduced profits. After eight years of struggling, he and his wife decided to leave the island and make a new start in Boston, Massachusetts. After failing at another business venture Parris began searching for a post as a minister in New England. Since he had not graduated from college, he knew he would not be eligible for a post in a major city.

Salem Village was the only parish that responded to Parris's application, yet he kept the community waiting for over a year while he deliberated (thought about) the offer. The delay resulted from his reluctance to lower himself socially as well as his fear of Salem itself. The village had a reputation for being a difficult place to live because of conflicts within the community. For instance, members of the Towne family were long-time enemies of the powerful Putnam clan, who were pressuring Parris to move to Salem. The feud had begun in 1639, when John Putnam started a dispute over rights to woodlands with his neighbor Jacob Towne. In retaliation (to get revenge) Towne cut down one of Putnam's trees. Putnam returned with a group of his relatives and threatened to cut down all of Towne's trees. Thus began a feud that lasted over fifty years.

Not only did family feuds run deep but Salem Village parishioners generally did not welcome outsiders and they mistreated their ministers. Since the founding of the parish in 1672 the Reverend George Burroughs and the Reverend James Bailey were both forced out of their jobs when the villagers refused to pay their salaries. (Burroughs would later be one of the twenty people executed in the Salem witch trials; see Chapter 4.)

Parris had extensive negotiations with the parish over money and property rights, asking for a high salary and a permanent title to the parsonage (the minister's home) and grounds. Despite the Putnams' assurances that Parris was a talented preacher, villagers dismissed his demands. Half of the townspeople felt he should receive minimum pay and no property rights, while the others were willing to make an investment in the new minister. In the end the Salem Village parish agreed to pay Parris the fairly large salary of sixty-six pounds a year and to give him temporary title (document stating legal ownership) to the parsonage. Many still felt this deal was too generous, however, and it later became an issue during the trials.

Parris had no choice but to accept the offer, so in November 1689 he and his wife arrived with their three children, Parris's eleven-year-old orphaned niece Abigail Williams, and the Carib (native South American) slaves **Tituba** (see biography entry) and John Indian. Parris took over the parish with such fervor that many villagers suspected him of being power-hungry. Unwilling to appease townspeople, he refused to ordain his deacons until they had served a probation period. He picked on respected members of the congregation and put some through public penance (punishment for sins) for seemingly ridiculous reasons.

Tensions in Salem Village

The Putnam family had been responsible for hiring Parris, and had done so in hopes of establishing a parish that was completely separate from that of nearby Salem Town. (Salem Village, near the Atlantic coast, was a bustling, densely-populated city. Salem Town, farther inland, was in a poorer, predominately agricultural area.) Many people in the Salem Village congregation were either Putnams or supporters of the Putnam effort to keep the village parish separate from the town. When Parris moved to Salem, the Putnams revoked (reversed) a 1681 agreement that the title to the parsonage would be held by the village rather than by an individual, thus granting him full rights to the land and the house. Tensions had already reached a peak over the issue of the title prior to Parris's arrival, and his presence only worsened the situation. Many villagers resented having to support a minister who had clearly aligned himself with the Putnams.

In 1691 five Parris supporters on the village governing committee were replaced by five anti-Putnam villagers who sought closer contact with Salem Town. Viewing the appoint-

ment of Parris as a political move on the part of the Putnams, the committee voted to not pay taxes (which paid Parris's salary) and not attend worship services at the meetinghouse. They also revoked Parris's ownership of the parsonage and the adjoining land. This was a financially devastating blow to Parris, who was now faced with the prospect of surviving entirely on voluntary contributions from the Putnams.

Fits and hallucinations

The final months of 1691 were a tense period in the Parris household. Not only was Parris's position in the community uncertain, but Elizabeth Parris was frequently ill. When she was well enough to go out, the Parrises were usually away from home on parish business. Thus the children spent most of their time with Tituba, who entertained them with stories about voodoo (magic) practices in Barbados. These forbidden tales contrasted starkly with the Bible stories and sermons the children were accustomed to hearing from Parris. As a strict Puritan, he considered all pleasure to be sinful and he tried to keep absolute control over the children. In January 1692 Parris's nine-year-old daughter Elizabeth (called Betty) and her cousin Abigail started behaving strangely and talking incoherently (in a confused and unclear way). (Records hint that there was deep psychological distress in the Parris children even before the witch trials.) The following month Tituba and John Indian baked a "witch cake" containing the girls' urine and fed it to the family dog in an attempt to identify whether or not any witches were casting a spell on them.

Soon, other girls in the neighborhood, including **Ann Putnam, Jr.** (see biography and primary source entries), had joined Betty and Abigail in having fits. They accused three women—Tituba, Sarah Osborne, and Sarah Good—of bewitching (casting a spell upon) them. In early March the women were taken to the meetinghouse for questioning, and during the investigation Tituba confessed to practicing witchcraft. Tituba, Good, and Osborne were all put in jail. By the end of May thirty-seven people had been arrested as suspected witches.

In the meantime Samuel Parris had taken control of the situation in his household. Alarmed that the devil had come into the very heart of the religious community, Parris knew events could easily be turned against him. His own slave, Tituba, had already admitted to being a witch, so he manipulated the crisis to his advantage by encouraging the girls to accuse other townspeople of practicing witchcraft. His plan was to divert attention away from his family and target members of the community whom he thought were trying to destroy him. In mid-March Parris sent Betty to live with the family of Stephen Sewall in Salem Town. (Sewall was the brother of **Samuel Sewall**, one of the judges in the Salem trials; see biography and primary source entries.)

Parris and the Salem trials

During the trials Parris aggravated tensions in the village by persecuting his parishioners and delivering sermons that encouraged anti-witch hysteria. In an especially damaging gesture, he excommunicated (expelled from church membership) accused witches Martha Corey and Rebecca Nurse, prominent members of the community who were eventually hanged (see Chapter 4 and primary source entry). When the elderly Nurse was in jail Parris gave a fiery sermon, "Christ Knows How Many Devils There Are," which contributed to the evidence against her. He also harassed relatives of accused witches. Parris's notes from that period show that he hounded Nurse's husband Sam to attend church when they missed even a single sermon. In the case of the Nurses, Parris clearly had political motivations: Nurse's maiden name was Towne, thus placing her in the anti-Putnam and anti-Parris camp, although there is no evidence that she was ever directly involved in the conflict surrounding Parris's appointment.

Parris also had a confrontation with Nurse's sister, Sarah Towne Cloyce, when Cloyce abruptly left a worship service, slamming the door behind her. From the pulpit Parris accused her of being yet another witch spreading evil among the good Christians of Salem. Her defenders asserted, however, that she had suddenly been taken ill and that a gust of wind had slammed the door as she left in haste. Cloyce was later arrested and found guilty of being a witch. As the trials continued through spring 1693, many were afraid to stop going to Parris's services and waited until the trials were over to drop out of the parish, but others risked being accused of witchcraft and simply stayed home.

Aftermath of the trials

Not only had Parris inherited an explosive position as the village minister, he had also encouraged the witch hysteria. When the trials were finally over, twenty people had been executed and many others had lost their property and reputations. Faced with a divided and bitter town, Parris was slow to address the central role he had played in the affair. Instead he chose to hide behind the excuse that the devil had been at work during that turbulent (unrestful) period. His behavior only intensified the deep hatred and tension in the village. Many people felt that as a leader he should not have allowed the trials to take place. The Nurse family was especially resentful of him, as he had done nothing to defend an innocent and beloved old woman. Two years later, in 1694, Parris finally offered an apology in a sermon, "Meditations For Peace," but it was not a heartfelt admission of error. He blamed the devil for being able to enter possibly innocent people and make them appear to carry out evil on his behalf:

> The matter being so dark and perplexed as that there is no present . . . appearance that all God's servants should be altogether of one mind in all circumstances touching the same, I do most heartily, fervently, and humbly . . . beseech pardon of the merciful God, through the blood of Christ, of all my . . . mistakes and trespasses in so weighty a matter, and also all your forgiveness of . . . every offense in this and other affairs wherein you see or conceive I have erred or . . . offended, professing in the presence of the Almighty God that what I have done . . . has been, as for substance, as I apprehended was duty. However, through . . . weakness, ignorance, etc., I may have been mistaken. (From Chadwick Hansen, *Witchcraft at Salem*.)

Forced out of Salem

Most of the people who had been ruined by Parris refused to attend his services during the trials, and they were determined not to return to church after the trials were over. Continuing to withhold all financial and public support from him, in 1695 they went before the governing council to seek formal conflict resolution with Parris. In diplomatic terms the council recommended that if Parris could not resolve his differences with the village he should leave, implying that he would not be dishonored if he choose to go. He refused to leave his post, however, and two years later he was again called before the council. This time the Inferior Court of the Common Pleas heard the case. The main complaints against Parris were that he had encouraged the girls' accusations and that he had forsaken (abandoned) his duties as a minister by not showing compassion for the victims of the trials. The court issued a statement that read in part:

> His believing the Devil's accusations and readily departing from all charity to . . . persons, though of blameless and godly lives, upon such suggestions; his . . . promoting such accusations; as also his impartiality therein in stifling the accusations of some and at the same time vigilantly promoting others . . . are just causes for our refusal. . . . Mr. Parris by these practices and principles has been the beginner and the procurer of the sorest afflictions, not to this village only but to this whole country that did ever befall them. (From Chadwick Hansen, *Witchcraft at Salem*.)

Reverend Green Starts the Healing Process

When Samuel Parris was forced to resign as the minister of Salem Village church and leave the community in 1697, he was replaced by the Reverend Joseph Green. More sophisticated and accepting than his predecessor, Green immediately tried to heal the community. He preached forgiveness in his sermons and even changed the seating arrangement in the church, forcing former enemies to acknowledge one another. He also brought justice to victims who had been ignored by the courts. In 1703 Green formally reversed Martha Corey's excommunication from the church, thereby restoring her reputation and assuring the relatives of other executed people that their loved ones would not be damned to hell. In 1712 he revoked (reversed) the excommunications of Rebecca Nurse and Giles Corey. Although Green's efforts eventually helped the community to recover from the devastation caused by the trials, Salem remained a symbol of fanaticism and injustice.

The judicial panel decided to bring an end to the matter, ruling that Parris should be discharged from his post but paid for his property and some of the salary he had lost. By this time Parris had little to lose. His wife had died the year before he lost his job, leaving him a widower. He had sold Tituba to another owner after the trials in order to pay her jailing fees and he had sent Abigail to live with other relatives during the trial. Parris left Salem with young Betty and his son Noyes, who had been named for a witch-hunting parson. Noyes lapsed into insanity during adulthood, and there is no record of what became of Betty, other than the fact that she eventually married and moved away.

Parris went on to another post in an even more remote village, Stow, Massachusetts, which had a population of only twenty-eight families. Located on the border of Native American territory, Stow had a history of troubles with Native Americans and years of poor harvests. Nevertheless, Parris again demanded a high salary and the deed to the parsonage. The people of Stow balked at his requests, and he was discharged within a year. Luckily, Parris had married a wealthy woman and spent the rest of his days in Boston, financed by his new wife's fortune. He tried his hand at several different careers, including teaching, farming, and running a shop, but he left enormous debts when he died in 1720.

For Further Reading

Hansen, Chadwick. *Witchcraft at Salem.* New York: George Braziller, 1969.

Hill, Frances. *A Delusion of Satan: The Full Story of the Salem Witch Trials.* New York: Doubleday, 1995.

Kallen, Stuart A. *The Salem Witch Trials.* San Diego, California: Lucent Books, 1999.

Rice, Earle, Jr. *The Salem Witch Trials.* San Diego, California: Lucent Books, 1997.

The Salem Witch Museum. [Online] http://www.salemwitchmuseum.com/ (Accessed July 7, 2000).

Starkey, Marion L. *The Devil in Massachusetts: A Modern Enquiry into the Salem Witch Trials.* New York: Doubleday, 1989.

Wilson, Lori Lee. *The Salem Witch Trials.* New York: Lerner, 1997.

John Proctor

Born: 1632
England
Died: August 19, 1692
Salem, Massachusetts

Farmer, tavern owner, and accused wizard

John Proctor was one of twenty people executed during the Salem witch trials in 1692–93. Condemned to death as a wizard (a man who practices magic), he was targeted by the court for expressing open opposition to the trials. Thus Proctor was doomed because of his own outspokenness. Yet he was also a victim of the accusations of his maidservant, Mary Warren, who belonged to the group of young girls who initiated the witchcraft charges that resulted in the mass hysteria.

John Proctor and Salem Village

John Proctor was born in England, and at an early age he emigrated to Ipswich, Massachusetts, with his family. In 1666 he moved to the outskirts of Salem Village, settling on a large tract of land he inherited (received ownership of) from his father and becoming one of the wealthiest property owners in the village. He and his wife Elizabeth also ran a tavern in Salem Town (the Salem community consisted of the larger, more urban Salem Town and the smaller, more rural Salem Village). As a successful farmer and businessman Proctor was envied by his village neigh-

Dorcas Good, Five-Year-Old Witch

In the early phase of the Salem trials, when young girls began accusing respected townspeople of being witches, many villagers were skeptical of their claims and rushed to defend the suspects. Yet within only a few weeks the testimony of a few witnesses swayed public opinion.

A particularly compelling witness was Dorcas Good, the five-year-old daughter of Sarah Good, one of the first three women accused of practicing witchcraft. Soon after her mother's arrest Dorcas confessed to being a witch herself. In court she spoke at length about having her own "familiar" (an animal that has been inhabited by a witch), a small snake that she claimed to nurse between her fingers. Upon examining her hands, court officials found a deep red spot on her forefinger—a sign that she was a witch. Although the spot could have been caused by a number of factors, the spectators needed no other evidence to convince them that Dorcas was telling the truth. When pressed to reveal who had given her the snake as a familiar, Dorcas shocked the audience by condemning her own mother. Her confession came only days after the controversial arrest of Rebecca Nurse, a beloved and respected member of the community. Fears of a widespread witches' conspiracy had been gaining momentum daily, so when the child revealed that she and her mother were witches, the community's worst suspicions were confirmed. Those who dared to question the arrests of suspected witches were immediately silenced.

bors and respected by the people of Salem Town. Although he was never directly involved in Salem Village politics (see Chapter 4), his tavern was located in the town and he therefore remained a target of suspicion in the divided community.

Proctor's troubles began when his sister-in-law Rebecca Nurse was arrested on March 19, 1693. His maidservant Mary Warren was one of several young girls who had recently joined Elizabeth (Betty) Parris, daughter of minister **Samuel Parris** (see biography entry), and Abigail Williams, Betty's cousin, in having fits (see Chapters 3 and 4). As the main accusers in the Salem trials, they had testified against Nurse in court (see primary source entry). The day after the arrest, Proctor went to the village to find Warren. According to *Witchcraft at Salem,* Proctor

Witches were thought to own strange, evil animals, or "familiars," that could help them bring harm to others.
Reproduced by permission of Pennsylvania State University.

was enraged by her behavior, and he publicly denounced all of the girls, charging that they were faking their fits: "If they were let alone we should all be Devils and witches quickly," Proctor exclaimed. "They should rather be had to the whipping post. . . . Hang them! Hang them!" According to witnesses he took Warren home and beat her until she regained her composure, then as she had more fits he beat her again. Villagers were shocked by his actions, which they considered brutal treatment of a defenseless, afflicted girl. Proctor had also endangered his own position in the village by making an untimely outburst early in the witch-hunt, when public opinion was shifting toward support of the accusers.

The Proctors are accused

Few villagers had dared to speak out against the trials, so Proctor had sealed his fate by publicly chastising (scolding) Warren for accusing innocent people of being witches. Elizabeth Proctor had been even more critical of the trials than her husband, but he had consistently supported her. On April 4, 1693, villagers Jonathan Walcott and Nathaniel Ingersoll entered official complaints against Elizabeth and Sarah Cloyce, Rebecca Nurse's sisters. The women were officially arrested on April 8 and interrogated (questioned) three days later. During a pre-trial examination the young accusers were unable or unwilling to answer questions about Elizabeth's involvement in witchcraft. Finally John Indian, a slave in the Parris household and husband of confessed witch **Tituba** (see biography and primary source entries), claimed that Elizabeth's specter (spirit) had tried to choke him. The girls sat silently until they were forced to speak. This time they put on a memorable show by going into such severe fits that trial judge **Samuel Sewall** (see biography entry) noted the event in his diary entry for April 11. As the girls thrashed about on the floor, they babbled incriminating evidence against Elizabeth. The most damaging accusation was that Elizabeth had forced Mary Warren to sign the devil's book and then had cast a spell on her. As stated in *Witchcraft at Salem*, Elizabeth replied "Dear child, it is not so. . . . There is another judgment, dear child." The word "judgment" sent the girls into another frenzy. Abigail Williams cried out that she saw Proctor's specter walking over to Goodwife (the Puritan term for a married woman) Bibber, one of the spectators in the courtroom—at which point Bibber herself went into fits. This spectacle was enough to doom Elizabeth, even though she was pregnant at the time and had been calm under questioning. John Proctor defended his wife in public and was immediately arrested for participating in witchcraft with her.

Proctor appeals for help

On April 11, 1693, the Proctors were taken to jail to await trial. Prior to their arrest a sheriff came to their home and, as stated in *The Devil in Massachusetts*, "seized all the goods, provision and cattle that he could come at, and sold some of the cattle at half price and killed others and put them up for [sale in] the West Indies; threw out the beer out of the barrel and carried away the barrel, emptied a pot of broth and took away the pot and left nothing for the support of the

Mary Warren Admits to Faking Fits

A possible reason that Salem villagers turned against the Proctors was John Proctor's treatment of their maidservant Mary Warren, one of the original accusers in the trials. He had beaten her and publicly chastised (scolded) her for targeting innocent people as witches. Although Warren initially hurled accusations with the same zeal and fervor as the other young girls, she eventually calmed down and went so far as to admit she had lied. Indeed, according to *The Devil in Massachusetts,* after one of her fits she confessed that "It was for sport." At this point Warren's fellow accusers turned on her, claiming she was working in league with the devil. When the Proctors were arrested as suspected witches, Warren did not dare to speak out against Proctor or his wife Elizabeth; she was known to be particularly fond of John, even though he had beaten her. For these reasons she found herself accused on April 19, 1693, shortly after her employers were arraigned for questioning. During Warren's interrogation, chief magistrate John Hathorne asked her why she had switched from accuser to accused. She replied, "I look up to God and I take it to be a great mercy of God." Hathorne immediately seized on her statement as a confession. Knowing she was trapped, Warren fell into fits and cried out, "I will Speak! . . . Oh I am sorry for it! I am sorry for it! Oh Good Lord save me! I will tell! I will tell!" She apparently lapsed into such a severe state that her jaws locked and she was unable to move or speak. Her affliction was interpreted as bewitchment by one of the accusing girls, who told the court that Elizabeth Proctor's specter had come to torture Warren.

Warren was taken to jail, where she was subjected to frequent questioning, always to the point of confession. In her confessions she condemned the Proctors as witches, but witnesses also took note of her calm and lucid (clear) state at other times, when she defended John in particular. On May 12, 1693, Warren stopped trying to defend John and told her jailers that she felt his shape hovering above her. She went into another severe fit, and this time her legs could not be uncrossed unless they were broken. Warren was allowed to go free and returned to the group of girls in the courtroom, but she never fully regained her sanity.

[Proctors'] children." On July 23, four days after the execution of Rebecca Nurse, Proctor asked his fellow prisoners to sign an appeal for help to Increase Mather (see Chapters 2 and 3 and primary source entry), **Cotton Mather** (see Chapters 2 and 3

The courts were overrun by accused witches, supposedly afflicted victims, and witnesses trying to save their friends and loved ones.

Reproduced by permission of the Peabody Essex Museum.

and biography and primary sources entries), and three other members of the Boston clergy. In the petition Proctor revealed two factors in the trials that he felt the ministers would find troubling. First, he wrote that his own son William had been tortured into accusing his parents of being witches. Village officials had tied William's neck to his heels until his nose bled and he finally confessed. Although this was strictly against New England law, which, according to *Witchcraft at Salem,* declared such actions "barbarous and inhumane," the practice was apparently becoming quite common. Physical torture was especially popular in the few cases where there was no free confession. Second, Proctor reported the extensive use of spectral evidence (that one's spirit had committed an evil deed), which the ministers had wanted to keep to a minimum in the trials because it could not be substantiated (proven) with concrete facts. Upon receiving the petition, they held a conference and finally decided not to pay attention to the plea. In a weak response to the charge about spectral evidence, the clergymen issued a statement in which they claimed it was occasionally possible for the devil to enter into people and make them do his work. The ministers also took no action to investigate the charges of torture, essentially turning their backs on Proctor. Increase Mather did write back, saying he would try to be at Proctor's trial, but he did not attend.

Proctor bravely faces death

Both John and Elizabeth Proctor were found guilty, and on August 5, 1693, they went to court to receive their sentences. Present in the courtroom were thirty-one of John's friends from Ipswich and twenty-one neighbors from Salem Village, who came to express their support. At the risk of being incriminated themselves, they had signed a petition declaring Proctor's innocence and citing his position as an upstanding member of the community. Their appeal had no effect on the courts, however, because the judges were already determined to see Proctor die:declaring him innocent at this point would have caused too many questions about other cases. John was condemned as a wizard and on August 19 was taken with five others to be hanged on Gallows Hill. Before being executed he made a final plea for justice. In the words of Thomas Brattle, a witness to the execution, Proctor and his fellow condemned prisoners:

> protested their innocency as in the presence of the great God whom forthwith they were to appear before. They wished, and declared their wish, that their blood might be the last innocent blood shed upon that account. With great affection they entreated Cotton Mather to pray with them. They prayed that God would discover what witchcrafts were among us. They forgave their accusers. They spake without reflection on jury and judges for bringing them in guilty and condemning them. They prayed earnestly for pardon of all other sins and for an interest

Many years later, the families of those who were sentenced to hang were given compensation for their losses.

Reproduced by permission of the Corbis Corporation (Bellevue).

in the precious blood of our Redeemer, and seemed to be very sincere, upright, and sensible of their circumstances on all accounts, especially Proctor and [John] Willard, whose whole management of themselves from jail to the gallows and whilst at the gallows was very affecting and melting to the hearts. (From Chadwick Hansen, *Witchcraft at Salem.*)

Although Elizabeth Proctor was also sentenced to die, she "pleaded her belly" (pregnancy) and was allowed to wait in jail until her baby was born; she finally received a pardon. Yet her husband had left her nothing in his will, so she was faced with the task of raising six children only on her barely cleared name.

Nearly two decades later the Proctor family did receive payment for the losses they incurred during the trials. In 1710 Salem villager Isaac Easty appealed to the court for compensation for the loss of his wife Mary, who was executed. As stated in *A Delusion of Satan*, acknowledging that nothing could make up for his "sorrow and trouble of heart in being deprived of her in such a manner," he delared that the courts should render justice to him and the families of other victims. Easty's action prompted relatives of executed witches Elizabeth Howe, Sarah Wildes, Mary Bradbury, George Burroughs, Giles and Martha Corey, and Rebecca Nurse to submit similar pleas. The courts granted a sum of 578 pounds (British money) to be split among the families of victims according to their financial status prior to the trials. According to *A Delusion of Satan,* the Proctors received 150 pounds, a major portion of the final settlement. In contrast, the family of Elizabeth Howe was awarded only 12 pounds.

For Further Reading

The Crucible. Twentieth Century Fox, 1998. Videocassette recording.

Hansen, Chadwick. *Witchcraft at Salem*. New York: George Braziller, 1969.

Hill, Frances. *A Delusion of Satan: The Full Story of the Salem Witch Trials*. New York: Doubleday, 1995.

Kallen, Stuart A. *The Salem Witch Trials*. San Diego, California: Lucent Books, 1999.

Rice, Earle, Jr. *The Salem Witch Trials*. San Diego, California: Lucent Books, 1997.

The Salem Witch Museum. [Online] http:// www.salemwitchmuseum.com/ (Accessed July 7, 2000).

Starkey, Marion L. *The Devil in Massachusetts: A Modern Enquiry into the Salem Witch Trials*. New York: Doubleday, 1989.

Wilson, Lori Lee. *The Salem Witch Trials*. New York: Lerner, 1997.

 The Crucible

John Proctor is featured as a main character in *The Crucible* (1953), a drama about the Salem witch trials by American playwright Arthur Miller. In the play, which has become a classic around the world, Miller examines the complex moral dilemmas confronted by Proctor, who is wrongly accused of practicing witchcraft. Through a depiction of the mass frenzy of the witch-hunts, Miller addresses the social and psychological aspects of group pressure and their effects on individual ethics, dignity, and beliefs. Although the plot and characters are based on transcripts of the trials, some of the facts have been altered for dramatic effect. *The Crucible* is frequently performed, and in 1996 the play was adapted as a feature film, with Daniel Day-Lewis starring as John Proctor and Winona Ryder as Abigail Williams.

Ann Putnam, Jr.

Born: 1680
Salem, Massachusetts
Died: 1717
Salem, Massachusetts

A main accuser in the Salem witch trials

Modern historians have portrayed Ann Putnam, Jr. as a victim of the Salem witch trials. Although she was one of the primary accusers who sent twenty innocent people to their deaths as convicted witches, she had been trapped in a vicious cycle of events caused in part by her parents. Her father, Thomas Putnam, was seeking revenge on his enemies in a long-standing land feud. Her mother, Ann Putnam, Sr., had become immersed in the occult (attempts to influence events through supernatural forces) as a way to avenge the death, years earlier, of her own beloved sister. Thirteen years after the end of the Salem trials, Ann, Jr. came forward as the only accuser to issue an apology to the families of the executed witches.

Influenced by parents' obsessions

Ann Putnam, Jr. was born in Salem Village, Massachusetts, and grew up in a tense and troubled household. For over fifty years her father's family had carried on a boundary dispute with their neighbors, creating deep divisions within the community. As owners of large tracts of land, the Putnams wielded considerable political power and they were leading a campaign to keep rural Salem Village separate from the more urban Salem Town. Their main strategy was to establish a church that was independent from the Salem congregation. In 1688, after two other ministers had been forced to leave their posts, Thomas Putnam and his relatives pressured the Salem Village congregation to hire **Samuel Parris** (see biography entry) as the new preacher. They also took the unusual step of giving Parris a high salary and granting him the title to (legal ownership of) the parsonage (minister's home) and surrounding land.

By the time Parris arrived the following year the community had broken up into two factions, those who supported the Putnams and his decision to hire Parris, and others who opposed the appointment of Parris. Soon the anti-Parris group gained enough votes on the village committee (local governing body) to withhold taxes that paid the minister's salary. This situation had a direct impact on the Salem trials of 1692–93, and on Ann, Jr., who became one of the main accusers of suspected witches (see Chapters 3 and 4). Most of the accused people belonged to or were associated with the anti-Putnam faction, and Thomas Putnam actively encouraged Ann to make accusations throughout the trials

Not only was Ann, Jr. caught in the middle of the Putnams' political battles, she was also pulled into her mother's obsession with the occult. Ann Putnam, Sr. moved to Salem Village as a teenager with her older sister Mary, who had married James Bailey, the first minister of the village parish. Mary suffered several failed pregnancies, eventually dying in childbirth. Ann, Sr. and Mary were extremely close, and Ann strongly believed that Bailey and the people of Salem Village were responsible for her sister's death. She felt that, as outsiders, she and Mary had been treated with such hostility that her sister was physically and emotionally exhausted to the point of death. Apparently Bailey was an ineffective leader of the village parish and his political enemies went out of their way to torment the perpetually pregnant Mary. Ann thought many villagers were pleased when Mary died, and she would hold a grudge against these people for many years to come.

Ann, Sr. was married to Thomas at age sixteen and, like Mary, she had several babies who died at birth. Finally, Ann, Jr.

was born in 1680, but Ann, Sr. continued to be haunted by the feeling that townspeople had been responsible for her family's misfortunes. She became so obsessed that she tried to communicate with Mary through occult rituals and thus lived a secretive double life. She eventually involved Ann, Jr. in this secret life. A well-read and intelligent child, the younger Ann was pushed by her mother into a level of maturity well beyond her years. Together they often visited the graveyard where Mary was buried, avidly reading the Book of Revelations in the Bible in search of clues for contacting the dead. In 1691 Ann, Sr.'s obsession with the occult reportedly led Ann, Jr. to **Tituba** (see Chapters 3 and 4 and biography entry), the Carib slave in the Parris household.

Joins Tituba's circle

Tituba had been entertaining Parris's nine-year-old daughter Elizabeth (called Betty) and his eleven-year-old niece Abigail Williams, who was also living in the home, with stories about voodoo (magic) customs in her native West Indies. Soon Ann, Jr. and other Salem Village girls had joined Tituba, Betty, and Abigail in the tale-telling sessions. At that time only twelve years old, Ann, Jr. had been sent by her mother to Tituba for advice in contacting the spirit of Mary Bailey. Ann, Jr.'s adult knowledge of the world had made her high strung and fearful, yet she became one of Tituba's best "pupils." She had a quick mind and an active imagination, as well as extensive experience with her mother's own brand of occult practices, which enabled her to understand Tituba's stories.

By January 1692 other neighborhood girls were gathering around Tituba at the Parris fireside. When Betty and Abigail fell into fits that month, Ann, Jr. and Elizabeth Hubbard, one of the other village girls, joined them in exhibiting extreme emotional distress and incoherent (confused and unclear) babbling. The following month Tituba and her husband, John Indian, baked a "witch cake" containing the girls' urine and fed it to the family dog in an attempt to identify the witches who were casting a spell on them. In February the girls accused three women—Tituba, Sarah Osborne, and Sarah Good—of bewitching (casting a spell upon) them. In early March the women were taken to the meetinghouse (church

Ann Putnam, Jr. Discovers Her Powers in Andover

Sometime before the first Salem trial executions took place in July 1693, the village of Andover, Massachusetts, was struck by the witch scare that was spreading like wildfire through the region. When the wife of Andover resident Joseph Ballard suddenly fell ill, Ballard immediately tried to determine the occult causes of her illness by sending for an accuser from Salem. This was how Ann Putnam, Jr. found herself, along with fellow accuser Mary Walcott, riding a horse to Andover to consult the sick woman and her relatives. The girls were welcomed as heroines, and they relished their virtually unquestioned power. They were taken through dozens of homes to visit sick patients and determine whether or not they felt the presence of a witch who could be held responsible for the afflictions. Since Ann and Mary did not know everyone in the village, they could not identify the witches' specters (spirits) they saw sitting by the patients.

The justice of the peace, Dudley Bradstreet, therefore arranged a sort of line-up to help solve the problem of anonymity. He mixed a group of suspects with respected citizens, blindfolded all of them, and had them walk individually past Ann and Mary as the girls were in the throes of possession. The people in the line-up were instructed to touch the girls' hands. If a girl stopped her fit for a moment then the person was considered guilty, as it was believed the person was calling off the demons and was thus in control of the situation. Bradstreet had not anticipated, however, that the girls would name many more people than he had hoped. By the end of the day Ann and Mary had identified more than half a dozen "witches," and forty warrants had been issued for arrests of other line-up participants. In fact, there were so many suspects that Bradstreet quit writing warrants. The accused were sent to the town jail to await trial without legal representation. Now even more confident of their powers, Ann and Mary returned to Salem to appear as witnesses in the trials. Ann was one of the main accusers who sent twenty innocent people to their deaths by September 22, 1693, when the last hangings took place.

building) for questioning, and during the investigation Tituba confessed to practicing witchcraft. Tituba, Good, and Osborne were all put in jail. Later that month Ann Putnam, Sr. was also having fits and led the girls in accusing Rebecca Nurse, a respected seventy-one-year-old member of the Salem Village congregation, of being a witch (see primary source entry). Sig-

nificantly, Nurse was a member of the Towne family, long-time enemies of the Putnams in the boundary feud. Formal witchcraft trials began, and by the end of May thirty-seven people had been arrested as suspected witches. Throughout the trials Ann, Jr. remained the most active accuser, often displaying the wildest behavior and hurling the most devastating charges at her victims.

The drama continues

Ann, Jr. was placed in the spotlight in September 1693, when Salem villager Giles Corey was arrested and charged with wizardry (practicing magic). Corey's wife Martha had already been sentenced to death. He refused to stand trial for his alleged crimes because, according to local law, a prisoner's property could not be confiscated (seized by authority) except in cases of treason or conviction. The law also held, however, that refusal to testify could result in being subjected to a slow death by crushing with heavy stones. In an effort to keep his property in his family and to avoid being convicted as a wizard, Corey submitted to being crushed by stones in a field outside Salem, where he finally died after nine days on September 19. Martha Corey was hanged three days later.

While Giles Corey was dying, Ann was at home claiming to experience the exact pain that he was feeling. Behaving as if she were under duress from a suffocating force, Ann was suddenly relieved of her pain when she saw the spirit of a witch who explained to her why Corey was now being crushed to death. According to the spirit, Corey himself had long ago crushed a man to death with his feet while under a contract with the devil. Part of the deal with the devil was that the murderer would profit from the man's death, but then would someday face the same fate himself. According to *The Devil in Massachusetts,* when Ann recounted this vision to her father, he suddenly recalled that seventeen years earlier, long before Ann was even born, Corey had been charged in court with the death of a man who was "bruised to death." He had somehow escaped justice in the courtroom and had never been found guilty. Putnam revealed this story to nervous villagers, who welcomed the news. Not only could they now have a clear conscience in putting Corey to death, but Ann's vision had given them proof that she was telling the truth. No one considered the fact that Ann's mother had told her about past events in Salem Village and had filled the child with bitterness toward certain residents.

Ann apologizes for role in trials

By October 1693 jails in the Salem area were packed with suspects, and twenty people had been executed as witches, largely at the urging of the young girls. Ann, Jr. and her friends had almost single-handedly devastated entire villages, at times even turning against their own—as in the case of former accuser Mary Walcott (see box on p. 216), who failed to cooperate in the trials (see Chapter 4) and soon found herself suspected of being a witch. Nobody had been safe from the girls' accusations and their frequent fits. In November, however, they discovered that they had lost their power when they were called to nearby Gloucester to determine why a soldier's sister lay ill. Although the girls named three culprits, the accused witches were not imprisoned. On their way home from this disappointing event, the girls were crossing Ipswich Bridge and went into fits while passing an old woman. To their astonishment, nobody paid them any attention and they were for once treated as if they were crazy or invisible. This was to be the last of their accusations and fits, and a solemn silence overtook all of them.

As the trials came to an end and the families of victims sought justice, the accusers slipped into uncomfortable obscurity. Most of the girls left Salem Village with their families or got married and later moved away, but Ann Putnam, Jr. stayed on. Both of her parents died within a week of one another at a relatively young age in 1699, leaving Ann to raise her nine younger siblings by herself. She remained anonymous until 1706, when she was urged to make a public apology for her role in the trials, which would be the only statement from any of the accusers. Parris had been forced to leave his post in 1698 (see Chapter 5) and the new Salem Village pastor, Joseph Green, was determined to make peace within his parish. He took many steps to help reconcile (restore friendship between) enemies and reach an understanding of past transgressions (violations). In 1706 Ann asked Green if she could rejoin the parish, and the pastor required her to make the apology, not only as a way to relieve her own guilt but also to make peace in the community. Green read her lengthy statement to a congregation that included relatives of many executed witches. Among them was the family of Rebecca Nurse. The primary accuser of Nurse, Ann had insisted on the old woman's guilt and was clearly responsible for her execution, which had even shocked mutual enemies in the village. It was clear that Ann's speech was addressed mainly to the Nurse family, but the words rang true to everyone who had lived through the trials and had lost loved ones or helped accuse innocent people. (See the primary source entry for the full text of Ann's apology.)

Ann claimed she had never willingly meant to harm anybody during the trials and she begged forgiveness from those she had inadvertently hurt. She did not confess to any direct malice or guilt, however, instead blaming her actions on a "great delusion of Satan," whom she held responsible for the witch-hunts. According to the account in *The Salem Witch Trials* by Earle Rice, Jr., she admitted only to the "guilt of innocent blood." Referring indirectly to the role of her own family in the social turmoil at the time of the trials, she said she "desired to lie in the dust and to be humbled for it, in that [she] was the cause, with others, of so sad a calamity to them and their families. " Ann lived for eleven more years, dying single and alone at the age of thirty-seven.

For Further Reading

Hansen, Chadwick. *Witchcraft at Salem.* New York: George Braziller, 1969.

Hill, Frances. *A Delusion of Satan: The Full Story of the Salem Witch Trials.* New York: Doubleday, 1995.

Kallen, Stuart A. *The Salem Witch Trials.* San Diego, California: Lucent Books, 1999.

Rice, Earle, Jr. *The Salem Witch Trials.* San Diego, California: Lucent Books, 1997.

The Salem Witch Museum. [Online] http://www.salemwitchmuseum.com/ (Accessed July 7, 2000).

Starkey, Marion L. *The Devil in Massachusetts: A Modern Enquiry into the Salem Witch Trials.* New York: Doubleday, 1989.

Wilson, Lori Lee. *The Salem Witch Trials.* New York: Lerner, 1997.

Samuel Sewall

Born: March 28, 1652
Hampshire, England
Died: January 1, 1730
Boston, Massachusetts

Businessman and public official

Samuel Sewall was a prominent businessman and judge in Boston, Massachusetts, during a time of social and political upheaval in the New England colonies. He is known today for making a dramatic public apology for the role he played as a judge in the Salem witch trials, which resulted in the executions of twenty people. Sewall is equally famous for his diary, a remarkable work that spans more than fifty years and provides modern historians with a vivid picture of life in Puritan New England. The diary offers an eyewitness account of the role of the Puritan elite in manipulating evidence in order to eliminate accused witches (see *Diary Entries and Apology of Samuel Sewall* in the Primary Sources section). After the Salem trials, Sewall went on to be a vocal advocate (supporter) of slaves' rights and tried to improve the living conditions of Native Americans.

Becomes Massachusetts judge

Samuel Sewall was born in Hampshire, England, on March 28, 1652, the son of Henry and Jane (Dummer) Sewall. When he was nine years old his parents moved to Newbury, Massachusetts, where he was educated at a private school. In

Samuel Sewall was the only judge from the Salem trials to offer an apology for his actions.
Reproduced by permission of Archive Photos, Inc.

1671 he graduated from Harvard College in Cambridge, Massachusetts, with a bachelors degree and three years later earned a masters degree from the same institution. Sewall was then ordained a minister, but he left the church to go into business when he married Hannah Hull in 1675. Sewall's father-in-law, John Hull, was the master of the mint (a government agency that prints money) for the Massachusetts Bay Colony and therefore had extensive connections in the business community. At Hull's urging, Sewall moved to Boston in 1681 to take over management of the colony's printing press. By the early 1690s he was a prominent figure in Boston business and political circles. He was a banker, publisher, international trader, and member of the colonial court. Although Sewall had no formal legal training, he also served as a judge (at that time a law degree was not required).

Sewall began his long career as a public official in 1683, when he was appointed to the Massachusetts General Court. The following year he was elected to the Massachusetts Council (governing body). While visiting England on business in 1684, he became involved in unsuccessful efforts to maintain the Massachusetts Bay Colony charter in its present form. Massachusetts Bay was the only self-governing English colony in America. Finally Britain revoked (canceled) the charter because Massachusetts Bay officials were illegally operating a mint. They were also basing voting rights on religious affiliation instead of property ownership and discriminating against Anglicans (members of the Church of England; the majority of the Massachusetts colonists were Puritans).

Presides at Salem trials

In 1691 Britain forced the Massachusetts Bay Colony to accept a charter that united it with Plymouth and Maine to form the Massachusetts colony. Under the new charter, church membership could no longer be a requirement for voting, although Congregationalism (a branch of Puritanism organized according to independent church congregations) remained the official church. Sewall was named a councilor (advisor) in the new royal government, a position he held until 1725, when he decided not to seek reelection. Historians note that the loss of the original charter led to widespread anxiety in Massachusetts, resulting in witchcraft hysteria. Puritan officials believed the colony was under an evil spell cast by witches (people, usually women, with supernatural powers) who had signed a compact (agreement) with the devil (the ultimate evil force). Witches were supposedly seeking revenge on particular members of the community. According to the Puritans, the compact empowered a witch to perform such acts as causing the death of a child, making crops fail, preventing cream from being churned into butter, or producing sterility (inability to conceive offspring) in cattle. They also believed witches inhabited the bodies of animals such as cats and dogs and became beings called "familiars," who could then prowl around and commit evil acts. The prominent Puritan leader Increase Mather wrote *Remarkable Providences,* a handbook on how to identify a witch, in 1684 (see primary source entry). He actively supported holding trials to rid the colony of witches.

In June 1692, when the Puritans decided to hold formal witch trials in Salem, Massachusetts, Governor William Phipps (1651–1695) appointed Sewall as a special commissioner (judge) on the court. Meeting in July and August, Sewall and the other judges interrogated (questioned) suspected witches and gave them a chance to reject their compact with the devil. If the suspects opened themselves to God, they would be reaccepted into the community. But many did not repent (feel regret for one's actions). The court ultimately sentenced twenty people, most of whom were women, to death. The executions were carried out in September: nineteen were hanged and a man was crushed to death. Almost immediately Sewall began to regret the role he played in this tragedy, and the guilt weighed increasingly upon his conscience. In fact, he felt he had greater responsibility in the matter than any of the other judges.

The Selling of Joseph

Samuel Sewall regretted his role as a judge in the Salem trials. Although he made a public apology in 1697, his involvement in sending innocent people to their deaths continued to weigh on his mind for the rest of his life. After the trials he appeared to develop a social conscience. He had long been troubled by the practice of slavery in the American colonies, but he had never taken the time to act on his views. Then, while he was serving as a judge in the Massachusetts General Court, he had to make a decision on a petition to free an African couple who were illegally held in bondage. Sewall therefore resolved to issue a public statement against the holding of African slaves. The result was *The Selling of Joseph* (1700), which is considered one of the earliest expressions of the abolitionist cause. The Joseph in the title is one of the heroes in the Book of Genesis in the Old Testament of the Bible. The favorite son of Jacob and Rachel, Joseph was sold into slavery by his brothers. They were jealous of his ambitions and the coat of many colors that Jacob had given to him.

In the opening of *The Selling of Joseph* Sewall argued that:

> originally, and naturally, there is no such thing as slavery. Joseph was rightfully no more a slave to [his brothers] than they were to him; and they had no more authority to sell him than they had to slay him. . . . 'Tis pity there should be more caution used in buying a horse, or a little lifeless dust, than there is in purchasing men and women.

Sewall went on to compare Joseph's situation with that of African slaves:

> It is likewise most lamentable to think how, in taking negroes out of Africa and selling of them here, that which God has joined together men do boldly rend asunder; men from their country, husbands from their wives, parents from their children. How horrible is the uncleanness, immorality, if not murder, that the [slave] ships are guilty of that bring great crowds of these miserable (unhappy) men and women [to America]. (From Giles Gunn, editor, *Early American Writing*, pp. 254–57.)

Develops a social conscience

By 1697 Massachusetts officials realized that the trials had been a terrible mistake, so the legislature designated January 14 as a special day of atonement (expression of regret and request for forgiveness). Taking this opportunity to make a public confession of his sins, Sewall wrote an admission of error and guilt. Then he stood and faced the congregation in the Old South Church at Boston as the Reverend Samuel

Willard read the statement aloud. As reprinted in *Early American Writing,* in the apology Sewall said he was taking "the blame and shame of it [the trials], asking pardon of men, and especially desiring prayers that God, who has an unlimited authority, would pardon that sin and all his other sins." Sewall was the only judge who publicly admitted his own guilt. Increase Mather and his son **Cotton Mather** (see biography and primary source entries), who were motivating forces behind the witch-hunts, eventually were instrumental in bringing the trials to an end. Yet the Mathers expressed their doubts only in published written works. Sewall continued to be troubled by his involvement in sending innocent people to their deaths. For the rest of his life he set aside a day of fasting a year to atone for his sins.

After Sewall made his public repentance he developed a social conscience, becoming active in abolitionist (antislavery) efforts. In 1700 he published *The Selling of Joseph,* an essay in which he argued against the keeping of African slaves (see box). Now considered one of the earliest antislavery statements, it is frequently reprinted in American history and literature texts. Sewall extended his concern to Native Americans, advocating that they be placed on reservations (lands set aside by the federal government solely for the use of different Native American peoples) and taught the language and customs of the English colonists. Colonial governments had been adopting this policy since the mid-1600s. Sewall's well-intentioned efforts were misguided, however, for the reservation system eventually resulted in the near extinction of the Native American way of life by the early nineteenth century.

Writes famous diary

Sewall wrote numerous historical and religious works as well as unpublished poetry during his lifetime. He is best known, however, for his diary, in which he gives a vivid picture of Puritan life in seventeenth- and eighteenth-century New England. (The diary spans the period from 1674 to 1729; there were no entries from 1677 to 1685.) Sewall was married three times. Hannah Hull Sewall, with whom he had fourteen children, died in 1717. In 1719 he wed Abigail Melyen, who died the following year. One of the most amusing passages in

Sewall's diary is his account of courting (seeking to marry) Katherine Winthrop, whom he hoped would become his third wife. He wrote that he gave her such gifts as sermons, gingerbread, and sugared almonds. Yet she would not be won over unless he promised to wear a wig and buy a coach. Finally unable to reach a marriage agreement with Winthrop, Sewall turned his affections elsewhere and, at age seventy, took Mary Gibbs as his third wife. He died eight years later, in 1730.

For Further Reading

Gunn, Giles, editor. *Early American Writing*. New York: Penguin Books, 1994.

Winslow, Ola Elizabeth. *Samuel Sewall of Boston*. New York: Macmillan, 1964.

Tituba

Date of birth unknown
Barbados, West Indies
Date and place of death unknown

Slave and accused witch

Tituba was a female Carib (Native South American) slave in the household of **Samuel Parris**, the minister of Salem Village church (see biography entry). She told voodoo stories to Parris's young daughter Elizabeth (called Betty) and his niece Abigail Williams. Betty and Abigail invited other local girls to join Tituba's storytelling circle, and before long all of the girls were lapsing into fits and accusing local residents of bewitching them. Many historical accounts credit Tituba's stories with starting the Salem trials in 1692–93. Nevertheless, Betty and Abigail also dabbled in childish magic tricks that were traditional to New England and not to Tituba's native Barbados, suggesting that these events may have occurred even without Tituba. When the girls started having fits it seemed natural for them to point an accusing finger at Tituba. Although it is not certain what her actual involvement was prior to this point, she played a central role in fueling the hysteria in the courtroom during the trials. Tituba was jailed as a suspected witch, but she was not executed, although twenty other accused witches were. She was released after a general reprieve of 1693, and Parris sold her to another owner in order to pay for her jailing costs.

Tituba and the Parris Family

Little is known about Tituba's life aside from her connection to the Parris family, primarily because she was a slave but also because she came from far-away Barbados. It is believed that Parris bought Tituba and her husband John Indian while living in Barbados in the 1670s. He took them to Boston, Massachusetts, in 1680 after his failed business attempts in Barbados convinced him to seek a job as a pastor in New England. Eventually he was hired to start a church in Salem Village. Tituba and John Indian moved to Salem with Parris in 1688 and were immediately considered outsiders in this small, isolated town where owning a slave, particularly a Carib rather than an African, was uncommon. Tituba and John Indian were given the majority of the indoor and outdoor chores of the household. Tituba was also in charge of caring for the children while the Parrises were making social calls in the parish.

Eight people shared the Parris home in Salem Village. The Parris family, which included two other children in addition to daughter Betty and cousin Abigail, and Tituba and John Indian all lived in a two-story, four-bedroom house that was rather large by local standards. Though the house was heated by a large central fireplace, winters were so cold that water would freeze on the hearth. Daily life was grueling, especially for the slave couple and the children. They would rise in the dark and gather to pray by the hearth. Breakfast was eaten by candlelight and then the work of the day began. Typical for the era, girls and women began with sewing, spinning, cooking, washing, and cleaning. Basically anything the family required for daily life was made at home, so days were filled with chores like making bread, butter, ale, clothing, candles, and other things. Men had no chores in the winter and were free to socialize. In the Parris home John Indian took care of any outside manual labor while Tituba tended to most of the indoor chores. The children took breaks only for meals at midday and evening and for nightly prayer sessions. Recreational activities and social visits were minimal for both slaves and children, for even when the weather warmed up leisure was considered sinful by Parris, a strict and pious (strongly religious) Puritan minister. (Puritans were a Protestant Christian group who believed in rigid social and religious rules.)

Girls target Tituba and others

With the Parrises frequently away from home, Tituba spent most of her time alone with the children. After long, tedious days they would often gather by the hearth to relax and tell stories. Tituba was a fascinating storyteller, and the children were fascinated by her tales of Barbados. The only other stories they ever read or heard were from the Bible (the Christian holy book), so these sessions by the fire were especially unique experiences for them. By late February 1693 several girls were being afflicted by hysterical fits and hallucinations. It is likely that their parents, and Samuel Parris in particular, urged or forced them to name certain people who were responsible for their behavior. Historians speculate that the pious and troubled Parris was eager to deflect the roots of this strange behavior out of his own household and onto others. Tituba and two village women, Sarah Good and Sarah Osborne, were the first three accused of being witches in the

Salem trials. Within days they were taken to the village for questioning by magistrates (judges) John Hathorne and Johnathan Corwin. This was a major event in Salem Village. Almost everyone took the day off to witness the court proceedings. The accused were brought through the village in a formal procession before being taken into an overcrowded, makeshift courtroom at a village inn. There was not enough space for everyone, however, as people had come not only from the village but also from the surrounding areas of Topsfield, Ipswich, Beverly, and Salem Town. The size of the audience forced local leaders to find a larger building, so they decided to use the church meetinghouse instead.

The officials and the girls were brought in first, then the church filled with people until every space was occupied. The room quieted as the first accused witches were brought to the front to be examined. Good and Osborne both spoke before Tituba and helped set the stage for her testimony. According to the court report, when Osborne was on the witness stand she spoke of possibly being bewitched (being under a spell) rather than being an actual witch. As described in *The Devil in Massachusetts,* she described seeing or dreaming "A thing like an Indian, all Black . . . [which] pinched her on her neck and pulled her by the back part of her head to the door of the house." By trying to deflect attention from herself onto the black man, Osborne inadvertently implicated herself as a witch (see Chapter 4).

Tituba confesses

According to records, Tituba had been severely beaten by Parris for several days before her appearance in court on March 1, 1693, and scholars conclude that he gave her instructions about what to say. When it was her turn to speak she told the audience exactly what they wanted to hear, but only after provocation (deliberately causing anger in someone) from Hathorne. The proceedings began with Hathorne's trademark style of questioning, which was relentless and emotional. He asked Tituba about her associations with evil spirits and she said she had none. As described in *A Delusion of Satan,* he then asked her why she was hurting the children and she answered, "They do no harm to me, I not hurt them at all." Ignoring her answer, Hathorne asked her why she had bewitched the girls, as if she had just confessed to a crime. She responded by saying again, "I have done nothing: I can't tell when the Devil works." Hathorne then pressed further by asking Tituba what connection she had to the devil and again demanding to be told who was hurting the children. To this Tituba replied vaguely, "The Devil for ought I know," which Hathorne chose to take as a confession. When he asked for a description of the devil or whoever was responsible for the bewitching, suddenly Tituba began to cooperate. Her demeanor (behavior) changed and she seemed to be trying to save her own life, which she knew was in danger. It was also commonly known that the only chance of escaping death during witchcraft charges was to confess.

According to *A Delusion of Satan,* Tituba started by admitting she had seen something "like a man," and the audience sat quietly as she described the devil himself. Spurred on by the reaction of the court, she admitted to being a witch, a fact that shocked the audience and sent the girls into hysterics. As described in *Witchcraft at Salem,* Tituba admitted that "The Devil came to [her] and bid [her] to serve him." She said the Devil had sometimes appeared as a tall man dressed in black with white hair, and other times disguised as an animal (called a familiar) such as a rat or a cat. According to *The Devil in Massachusetts,* he said he was God and requested her service for six years: "He tell me he God and I must believe and serve him six years . . . the first time I believe him God he glad." He had brought her the witches' book in which she had entered her name and seen the names of nine other people, two of whom were Good and Osborne. Tituba claimed she had ridden with the women on a broomstick to a strange place and described the familiars the women had with them. One was a yellow bird that sucked Good's hand and the other had wings and legs but the head of a woman.

Confirms girls' accusations

In giving these details, Tituba was confirming the earlier testimony of the afflicted girls, who had described these very creatures. She also said that Good and Osborne had forced her to pinch the girls, whom she would never willingly harm, and that

Tituba Tries to Spare John Indian

When Sarah Osborne complained of having seen something "like an Indian" that had tormented her, the public imagination could certainly have turned to John Indian as the spectral culprit. This could have led to his arrest and death, but surprisingly he was never questioned for anything other than his own fits. He started having fits directly after the first hearing in the Salem trials, probably to deflect the attention away from himself as a possible culprit. John Indian was saved, however, when his wife Tituba focused attention on Sarah Good and Sarah Osborne with her fantastic descriptions of their activities together. Tituba's skillfully told tale prevented her husband from being imprisoned or in any other way affected by charges of witchcraft.

the women had helped the devil bully her into these acts. Tituba went so far as to say the women had come to her as specters (spirits or demons) and forced her to try to kill one of the main accusers, **Ann Putnam, Jr.** (see biography and primary source entries), with a knife. A few days earlier Putnam had spent hours in convulsions, screaming that someone was trying to cut her head off with a knife. Though nobody had been able to see this force, Tituba's words were confirming Putnam's experience. This statement sent the girls into violent fits, and when Tituba was questioned about who was afflicting them she accused Good. Confirming her accusation, the girls fell into even wilder convulsions. Then Tituba claimed to have been struck blind, a common sign of a witch renouncing (rejecting) her calling.

What happened to Tituba?

Tituba's confession may have saved her own life but it did not prevent the tide of future accusations. After the first interrogation, more and more people throughout the region were being accused of witchcraft. Tituba's words had confirmed Salem's deepest fears about the existence of evil in their midst. It had also sealed the fate of Osborne and Good, who were eventually executed. Tituba's suggestion that she had seen other names in the devil's book only heightened the hysteria. She was never again questioned in court or brought to trial, but sat languishing in a jail cell until May 1693, when Massachusetts governor William Phipps (1651–1695) ordered all accused witches remaining in jail to be set free. Prisoners were responsible for their own jailing fees, and since Tituba was Parris's property, her fees were his to pay. Parris sold her to another slave owner to recover his expenses, but records do not give any details about her life after that.

For Further Reading

Discovery Online—A Village Possessed: A True Story of Witchcraft. [Online] http://www.discovery.com/stories/history/witches/witches.html (Accessed July 7, 2000).

Hansen, Chadwick. *Witchcraft at Salem.* New York: George Braziller, 1969.

Hill, Frances. *A Delusion of Satan: The Full Story of the Salem Witch Trials.* New York: Doubleday, 1995.

Kallen, Stuart A. *The Salem Witch Trials.* San Diego, California: Lucent Books, 1999.

Rice, Earle, Jr. *The Salem Witch Trials.* San Diego, California: Lucent Books, 1997.

The Salem Witch Museum. [Online] http://www.salemwitchmuseum.com/ (Accessed July 7, 2000).

Starkey, Marion L. *The Devil in Massachusetts: A Modern Enquiry into the Salem Witch Trials.* New York: Doubleday, 1989.

Where to Learn More

Adler, Margot. *Drawing Down the Moon: Witches, Druids, Goddess-Worshippers, and Other Pagans in America Today.* Boston, Massachusetts: Beacon Press, 1986.

Barstow, Anne Llewellyn. *Witchcraze: A New History of the European Witch Hunts.* San Francisco, California: Harper, 1999.

Buckland, Ray. *Witchcraft From the Inside.* St. Paul, Minnesota: Llewelynn Publications, 1995.

The Crucible. Twentieth Century Fox, 1998. Videocassette recording.

Demos, John Putnam. *Entertaining Satan: Witchcraft and the Culture of Early New England.* New York: Oxford University Press, 1982.

Discovery Online—A Village Possessed: A True Story of Witchcraft. [Online] http://www.discovery.com/stories/history/witches/witches.html (Accessed July 7, 2000).

Hansen, Chadwick. *Witchcraft at Salem.* New York: George Braziller, 1969.

Hill, Frances. *A Delusion of Satan: The Full Story of the Salem Witch Trials.* New York: Doubleday, 1995.

Kallen, Stuart A. *The Salem Witch Trials.* San Diego, California: Lucent Books, 1999.

Ontario Consultants on Religious Tolerance. [Online] http://www.religious-tolerance.org/wic_rel.htm (Accessed July 7, 2000).

Rice, Earle, Jr. *The Salem Witch Trials*. San Diego, California: Lucent Books, 1997.

Rinaldi, Ann. *A Break with Charity: A Story about the Salem Witch Trials*. New York: Harcourt & Brace, 1994 (fiction).

The Salem Witch Museum. [Online] http://www.salemwitchmuseum.com/ (Accessed July 7, 2000).

Starkey, Marion L. *The Devil in Massachusetts: A Modern Enquiry into the Salem Witch Trials*. New York: Doubleday, 1989.

Stern, Wendy. *Witches: Opposing Viewpoints*. San Diego, California: Greenhaven Press, 1995.

Three Sovereigns for Sarah. PBS Home Video, 2000. Videocassette recording.

Wilson, Lori Lee. *The Salem Witch Trials*. New York: Lerner, 1997.

Wizards and Witches. Lehan, Brendan, and others, eds. Alexandria, Virginia: Time-Life Books; school and library distribution by Silver Burdett, 1984.

Index

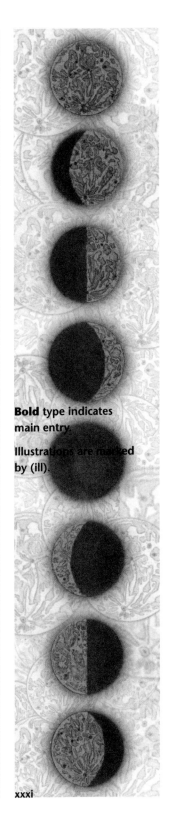

Bold type indicates
main entry.

Illustrations are marked
by (ill).